LIFE'S WORKBOOK

How to Write Your Autobiography Through Memoir Writing

A Life Calendar

100 Topics – Guiding Questions

A-Z Tool Sheets

CHARLOTTE DONALDSON

Life's Workbook – How to Write Your Autobiography Through Memoir Writing
Copyright 2017 by Charlotte Donaldson
Published by Zarrika LLC

Charlotte is also offering classes based on this book.
To reach Charlotte
LifesWorkbook@gmail.com
www.CharlotteDonaldson.com

Thank you, Bob Sarnoff & the late Maureen Daly McGivern, for encouraging me to complete this book. Thank you to my daughter Meredith Donaldson Amenkhienan for helping me with details during the last month.

Edited and formatted by Tom Sullivan from CambridgeEditors.
Edited also by Paulette Dusossoit, Jennie Shurleff Amirkaee, and Carol Savery-Frederick.
Cover and back design by Jerry Madara.
Front cover photograph by Charlotte Donaldson
Author's photograph by Richard Martin Davis.

Printed in the United States of America.

ISBN-13: 978-0692870457

DEDICATION:

This book is dedicated to my daughters—Hilary, Meredith, Tina, Opal, and Sheila—and all individuals who have chosen to explore their lives through this book. Enjoy the journey!

FOREWORD

The American writer, teacher and mythologist, Joseph Campbell described a format called **The Hero's Journey**, which is common to myths, legends, folklore, novels, and movie scripts. The four-stage pattern is that first something happens to upset a person's current level of functioning. Secondly, he goes on a journey to re-balance or adjust to the new situation. Thirdly there is a crisis, or series of crises, that usually get progressively worse until there is a climax. Finally, in the fourth stage or a resolution takes place.

The story line in a musical follows such a formula. (1) Boy meets girl and boy loses girl (2) Boy begins a journey to win her back, (3) There is a crisis that interferes with winning her back which gets even worse –until (4) A resolution, commonly their marriage. The story of *Cinderella* fits the pattern.

Another example is of *The Wizard of Oz*, in which, as Dorothy comes of age, she must find and embrace the various parts of herself including the Scarecrow/thinking part of her, the Tin Man/feeling part of her, and the Lion/acting part of her. The crisis in the narrative culminates the Wicked Witch of the West's evil and the disclosure of the Wizard's duplicity. Fortunately, there is a resolution when Dorothy's self-discovery and finding her way home.

These stories will live on as long as people continue to come of age and to fall in love. That is to say, psychologically, humans follow these patterns and pass them on to their descendants.

Charlotte Donaldson's *Life's Workbook - How to Write Your Autobiography Through Memoir Writing* acknowledges Campbell's theory and offers a practical means of helping readers to capture and pass the stories of their journeys to future generations. Doing so is an exercise in mindfulness. As you travel on a train looking out the window, you may see interesting scenery and events but never think of them until someone or something reminds you of having seen them. Similarly, one forgets the names of one's high school classmates unless one comes across a yearbook that lists them. This workbook serves a similar function, providing guiding questions that trigger not only remembrances of life's moments, but also insights into them.

The wonderful part of the workbook is that, like psychotherapy, it adapts to the reader's current level of insight, whatever it may be! That is to say, premature interpretations in psychotherapy are a negative, and the therapist must be responsive to whatever the patient's level of insight happens to be. This workbook allows for that.

It also acknowledges that at different ages people will have different levels of insight. I personally have found that in my retirement it's much easier for me to look back at my life objectively and to enjoy my successes and to be able to forgive my mistakes.

Mark Weiss Shulkin, MD
Associate Professor of Psychiatry Emeritus
Drexel University School of Medicine, Philadelphia, PA

TABLE OF CONTENTS

Detailed Contents

INTRODUCTION:

WHAT PROMPTED ME TO WRITE THIS BOOK?

I started writing this book when I was 29 (never mind how long ago that was!). It was then I started taking a more serious interest in my family's genealogy. Either there was little to no information, or what I did find had no heart and soul to the content. Recently, I have found two of my mother's scrapbooks. Going through these and discovering personal things about my family that I previously had no knowledge of was such a wonderful experience. This experience ignited my thinking about what I was leaving behind for my descendants.

Years ago a dear friend of mine died, leaving behind two toddler sons. There would always be facts and stories from other family members, but they would never know her genuine essence. Being a single mother of two toddlers myself, I was concerned I might pass and my children would not know my essence, thus I was more encouraged to write my autobiography.

With these motivations, I decided to start writing about my life. I found it hard to know where to start. Thinking about what I wanted to leave for my family, I started writing my own workbook to pull from. Afterwards I decided to write it for others, for the world.

Investigating one's life and family can reveal the most surprising information. This workbook includes charts, questions, exercises, and word associations all to help get to the nature of who you are. These activities will elicit this kind of information—the little things that make the difference between *knowing about* someone and *knowing* someone.

Many people have the desire to write their autobiography or a memoir, but few end up writing much of anything, and even fewer create a finished product. I believe it is because the task is overwhelming in the format of one chronological story. Most do not even get started. For that reason, this workbook's purpose is to get you over the first hurdle and Write Right Now! Whether you have been studying the art of writing memoirs and creating an autobiography or simply picked this book up because you liked the title or cover design, this may be the first step in a journey of discovery about yourself, your past, and the world in which you have lived. Do you want to preserve a record of your life for your family? Do you want to write a popular and potentially profitable memoir? Do you wish to revisit your past with an objective perspective, seeking clarification and/or healing? Whatever particular goal you have for your writing, this workbook can help you get started.

How does this book differ from other books on writing a memoir or an autobiography?

The difference between this book and most other books on writing is its focus on getting started. While most books on writing place the emphasis on the end product (particularly polishing your prose and getting published), this book emphasizes the process of creating your memoirs. This book can help you turn writing and thinking about your life into an **autotelic experience**[1]—that is, an experience that has an end or purpose in itself.

---

[1] Autotelic experience has been highlighted by the work of Hungarian psychologist Mihaly Csikszentmihalyi, and his theory of flow has profoundly influenced modern psychology. See Karen Stansbury Beard, "Theoretically Speaking: An Interview with Mihaly Csikszentmihalyi on Flow Theory

Most other books on memoir/autobiography focus on the practice of crafting a best-selling book or otherwise improving a body of already-written work. By contrast, this book's primary goal is to get you to Write Right Now! There are tools out there to help you if you want to get published, but for many people just having any sort of record for posterity is a step in the right direction.

The format is flexible and approachable no matter what your mood, your time constraints, or your level of uncertainty. Think of this book like you would view the menu at a restaurant. You choose what appeals to you at the time and only that. You can come back many times and have a different experience each time by trying a new dish. You may simply open a page and feel, "This is where I am supposed to be!" and start there. *The flexibility of this book is its beauty.*

Who would benefit from using this book?

This book is designed primarily for people ages twenty-five and older. It is designed so that you can write about one aspect of your life at a time, thus reducing the complexity and removing the stress of trying to create one long, continuous story. Also, you can answer the same questions at different times (say with a year or a decade between) and find that your answers change as you do. For example, if you just went through a difficult time in your life, you may have so much anguish and pain that you will write about the pain you are carrying or about the difficult time. Yet, at a later time, you may have forgiven (I did not say forgotten) the person or learned many lessons. When you reflect on the events, there is

---

Development and Its Usefulness in Addressing Contemporary Challenges in Education," *Educational Psychology Review*, 27(2015): 353–364.

more room for clarity and for humor because you are standing on the outside looking in rather than looking from the inside outward.

I suggest that you write about both recent events and the distant past. Sometimes I miss writing from that in-the-moment perspective. Now, I have many writings, and I refer to them to get back to those feelings. This way I can write and tell about the pain and the feelings I once had and that I have since let go. As you generate your own body of writings, you will be able to do the same, drawing from a well that gets deeper and richer as you go.

Can an amateur do this? What about a busy parent, adult, or professional?

If the concept of writing your autobiography feels too overwhelming or you think you do not have the time, let me ease your concerns. This book is custom designed for you. Rather than telling one long, sequential story, you will be prompted by specific questions, creating memoirs. *You will find yourself writing answers to questions you never knew to ask.* This is a *guide for writing an autobiography*; it is a *workbook* too. As you gather information, answer questions, and write from your heart, you will find yourself reflecting on many aspects of your life. As you remember poignant moments, a memoir will begin to develop. It will take passion, curiosity, and determination, and you will laugh, cry, and surprise yourself along the way.

What purpose does a memoir or autobiography serve?

By writing memoirs or creating an autobiography, you will have created a record of your life, a trove of source material for future writing, and materials for sharing, enjoyment, or meditation. Consider the vast amounts of information and knowledge you have collected over the years. Think of the little bits of wisdom that you may have obtained. What kind of knowledge do you have about your family, and what would be forgotten if you did not record it before your death? What do you want your family to learn about the life you have lived? Taking the time and effort to collect this information can be personally rewarding and also a great value to others. What a glorious gift you will have to share with your family and future generations. Each person who reads your story will feel more fulfilled knowing about their personal family history or the experiences of a fellow traveler in the great journey of life.

Try to remember what you know about an ancestor who you never met personally, like a great-great grandfather. Most of us are lucky if we have the basic facts of that ancestor's life and have no real idea what that person was like or who that person was on a personal level. Now imagine being able to read your great-great-grandfather's personal memoirs. Imagine what a gift it would be to know not just the how and where of his life, but also his habits, personality quirks, aspirations, trials, and acquired wisdom.

If you are a very private person or have no remaining family, then write for yourself. Discover your life from many different perspectives like a kaleidoscope, which shows changing images as the viewer's perspective changes. Our life's journey is about where we have been, where we are, and where we want to be in future years. *It is also about how we choose to interpret our experiences*. You can use this workbook to make sense of your past and present, and also to turn your eyes to the future. Your life is a moment in *social history* that will never repeat itself.

When you relieve the pressure of trying to create a publishable work, you create the freedom to enjoy the experience, to have an autotelic experience. This book will help you record your family roots, customs, personalities, lifestyles, humor and sadness, challenges, loves, hates, and indifference. Whether you publish your story for the world or pass fragments on to your kin, you'll create a valuable record of your life.

WRITE RIGHT NOW!

HOW TO USE THIS BOOK

This workbook is designed as a modular guide to getting started writing about your own life. The idea is to make writing about your life a rewarding experience in and of itself—an autotelic experience—and to remove the pressure of worrying about the final product. The materials can be used in any order, allowing you the freedom to follow your own inclinations. Just find a question or topic that interests you and start writing. There are hundreds of questions. If you do not like a question, then merely put a line through it and go on to the next one.

With this workbook, you will create an abundance of information for your family history from medical facts and photographs, to questions that prod you to think about your life from creative perspectives, illustrating even more of your personality.

As you write and collect a body of writings, you may decide that you wish to polish and publish them, either as a limited run for your own family or as a traditionally published book for the mass market. If you decide on one of these courses of action, there is a wide selection of other books that can help you navigate the various steps of revising, editing, and publishing your work.

What is in this workbook?

This workbook has three parts, each of which can be worked through in any order. The first part is a CHRONOLOGICAL CALENDAR OF YOUR LIFE, an activity to clarify the basic facts of your life. It will help you to remember the people who have been in your life, even if for only a short time. Some of them may help you recall poignant moments or intriguing stories. The next part contains 100 TOPIC QUESTIONS prompting you to get started and Write Right Now! In addition, the third part contains 26 TOOL SHEETS, lettered A–Z, to help you gather and record factual information. There is no set order in which to use the TOOL SHEETS and TOPIC QUESTIONS. You will find that several TOPIC QUESTIONS overlap with each other or with those found in the TOOL SHEETS. When this happens, just continue to write. You may gain a new perspective by responding to a different prompt—and therefore may write about the same memory in another light as it comes to mind. Do not resist or over-analyze the situation. Think of it as a kaleidoscope of your life—your life seen from many perspectives.

What can be done to ensure success with this workbook?

Effort and enjoyment are the keys to success. Relax and enjoy the experience, and trust that the activities themselves will eventually be rewarding—autotelic—even if you struggle early on. Choose the topics that appeal to you. If one exercise feels overly challenging, try a different one.

Through the methodology presented here, you will encounter one memory after another. *It is important to remember, when you have a recollection, to immediately jot down the name or the thought it brought to mind.* Keep a small notebook with you to help you collect your thoughts or use your cellular device to type or dictate your notes. It is best to enter a sentence rather than a word or phrase so you can return to finish your thought or continue writing when time allows.

Be as honest as you can. Write often. Perhaps take a vacation with this book and have a wonderful time wandering down memory lane. Allow yourself to come back and redefine or rewrite at a later date. If some parts are too emotional, wait to digest them and return later.

Each time you write, record the current date, the time of the event or your age at the time. You can start to organize your memoir manuscript in either topical or chronological order. You might even put an "*" in your Chronological Calendar of the date of the event you wrote about so you can choose to either have your book by topic or in sequential order.

You might consider creating an autobiography club with family or friends to give support and share some of your experiences or writing thrills and challenges with others.

Some of your memories will be from long ago and seem vague or unclear. You can help yourself remember by finding a quiet place to meditate, close your eyes, and take deep, slow breaths. Picture yourself as that long-ago person at that time and place. Use all five senses (taste, sight, sound, touch, and smell) to help bring the best light on the situation. Also you may include a sixth sense if it applies to the situation, like telepathy or extrasensory perception (ESP), or the less known equilibrioception (sense of balance) and proprioception (sense of body position).

The main way to ensure success is to dedicate time to work on the exercises. You may want to schedule a time each day to write. If you are not able to do that, then have an established time weekly when you take time for yourself and use this workbook. Set goals for yourself. Share with your family what you are doing. Perhaps you can have a family evening where everyone is working on his or her own autobiography at the same time.

Most importantly, get started! Flip through the TABLE OF CONTENTS and the worksheets until you find what feels like the perfect place to start. START THERE!

I highly suggest that you start with the CHRONOLOGICAL CALENDAR OF YOUR LIFE to form an overview of your life. This is a wonderful way to see how your life story fits together in chronological order. You will remember people, places, and events you have not thought about in years. Your life will come alive like an orchestra playing a symphony.

Let the questions catalyze your memories. Just start to write, draw, or doodle, but get started. *Time is a rare commodity that we can never regain once the moment has passed.*

WRITE RIGHT NOW!

Keep these key ingredients in mind, and soon you'll be creating your own memoirs.

$$TPT = Time \times Passion \times Truth$$

What You Will Need

Physical Tools

1. A computer or notepaper with three-hole paper or print on pre-punched three-hole paper. You can also use a hole punch later.

2. A three-ring binder.

3. Good pens (blue or black indelible ink ballpoint pens or permanent fountain pen ink is recommended because they do not bleed and copy well).

4. Pencils and a good eraser (for the CHRONOLOGICAL CALENDAR).

5. 1–100 numbered tab dividers (Avery Legal Exhibit Dividers #11370). You can use these 100 tabs in one of two ways. You can put the answers for the 100 TOPICS under their corresponding numbers. You can also organize your memoirs by your age (1–100) at the time of the events, corresponding with your CHRONOLOGICAL CALENDAR. This would keep your entire collection of work in chronological order.

6. A–Z lettered tab dividers (Staples #13498)

7. A small notebook to carry with you, to record ideas that may pop up at any moment.

8. A large bin or box to hold miscellaneous records and documents (Be sure to record the date and any other helpful information on each item):

   • Articles saved or obtained from the library or Internet of events that pertain to your family and poignant current events in your life.

   • Accounting information, such as old checks, bills, etc.

   • Calendars

   • Childhood clothing, baby blanket, or stuffed animals

   • Diaries

   • Journals

   • Letters

   • Photographs and videos (home movies)

   • Receipts from plays, air travel, hotels, ...

   • Recordings

   • Report cards

   • Scanned items, such as news articles and more

   • Souvenirs

   • Test results

- Writings you or your family have written or cherish

- Your accounting information to get details of events and costs

9. Markers, colored pencils, or highlighters. Establishing a color coding system can be helpful. For example:

  - RED – Stop. Topic highlighted to come back to later or too emotional for now

  - GREEN – Go. Completed for now

  - BLUE – Flood. Your idea flooded into another topic to be addressed later

  - ORANGE – Caution. Need more information such as writings, photos, research, etc.

  - PURPLE – Refined and completed

If you are more comfortable using a computer, you may prefer to do the activities in digital format. Even if you elect to complete the writing prompts electronically, you may still want to print out pages and put them in a traditional book format or binder for editing purposes. Likewise, keeping the box or file of physical materials is useful no matter what writing tools you choose.

Electronic Tools

1. Video camera

2. Camera

3. Audio recorder

Many will find the tools of a typical smartphone adequate for these purposes; of course, by all means use tools that are available and that you are comfortable with. Make it a habit to carry a camera or cellphone and take pictures of things that are a part of your daily life (save them regularly to a hard drive, thumb drive, or cloud storage in case you lose the device). Take pictures of where you live and what you experience seeing in a typical day, including vehicles and pets. Take pictures of your friends and professional colleagues. If you are simplifying your life, or before you sell something you feel sentimental about, take pictures of your sentimental items. Photos are a great way to record your life from the smallest to the largest memories. Record conversations with friends and family (but get permission to record first—it's illegal to record others secretly). Perhaps you will want to download any great voice messages you have received on your cell phone or answering machine. It can be wonderful to hear a voice from the past. Take videos of the most mundane happenings in your life. Someday, even these humdrum images will garner interest.

Online Tools

You can download the CHRONOLOGICAL CALENDAR OF YOUR LIFE (see www.CharlotteDonaldson.com) on your computer or print them out yourself or at a local printer or office store. You could add a stock board cover or put them into a spiral binder. I recommend choosing a larger 11 × 17 ledger/tabloid-sized paper.

The Objective: A Revised Philosophy on Writing

While some would like their writing to be easy and painless—automatic, so to speak—I think that writing ought to be difficult to a certain extent, a struggle. But that does not mean the struggle cannot be enjoyable. Just as many people learn to enjoy running for the experience and not just improved health, you can also learn to enjoy writing. An autotelic experience of writing is possible with a changed perspective. For many, this changed viewpoint is revolutionary.

My hope is that this book will nurture a positive attitude to enjoy writing with no grades, no teachers, no time restrictions, merely writing from your heart.

WRITE RIGHT NOW!

PART I: CHRONOLOGICAL CALENDAR OF YOUR LIFE

This is the most important step of this book. This of all things will bring memories and place them in chronological order as you experienced them. You might say that you have lost memories from your childhood. If you are still able to ask your parents, they might help you, or you can talk with your siblings or best friends. However, I can assure you that if you start this process you will be amazed at the recall you do have.

You can ask your local printer or office store that offers these services to print the calendar into a 100-page spiral bound notebook. You can ask them to format it with a color poster board cover too. To find the layout go to www.CharlotteDonaldson.com.

Use a pencil as you flip through the pages and jot down your thoughts. You will remember things about your childhood you have not thought about in ages—from people to adventures to all sorts of happenings. It will be the most *awakening* piece of this entire book.

Once you have filled out this calendar, you should consider writing in ink or using a spreadsheet format on the computer. Pencil will fade or smudge over the years, but it can be preserved with a thin coat of hair spray.

Note: For the first year of your life, you will enter year/age as the year you were born and age = 0.

Life's Chronological Calendar

Yr./Age	Jan	Feb	Mar	April	May	June	July	Aug	Sept	Oct	Nov	Dec
Home												
Address												
Family												
Health												
Education												
Work												
Travel												
Animals												
Events												

PART II: 100 TOPICS – GUIDING QUESTIONS

1: ACHIEVEMENTS, AWARDS, & PRIZES

ACHIEVEMENTS

What are the major achievements you have made in your life? (See TOPIC 24: DECADE DECALS).

AWARDS & PRIZES

What awards, honors, medals, prizes, or drawings have you won? Explain when this occurred, what year, the location, your age, for what occasion, and some memories. Were there some achievements that you wanted to make but did not? Were any undeserved? What made those you got special? Photograph your rewards and include them in your book.

SUCCESS/FAILURE

What has been and is now your definition of success and/or failure? What have been your greatest successes and failures? What have you learned? What advice or suggestions do you have for others?

RAFFLES

What raffles have you entered? Did you win any? If so, what did you receive as your prize? How old were you and where were you?

LOTTERY

Have you imagined winning the lottery? Did (or do) you buy lottery tickets? What are your thoughts about lottery tickets? Do you have family, friends, or acquaintances who have won the lottery?

WINNINGS & BETTING

What are your thoughts and feelings about betting? What winnings have you had? What bets did you lose? Explain what the outcomes were.

2: ADDICTIONS & SUBSTANCE ABUSE

Many people's loved ones become involved with drugs, either prescription or illegal. Since I started writing this book, the abuse of opioids, including prescription pain medication like oxycodone and heroine has become epidemic. Many times, troubles begin after an event as innocent as a high school sports injury, followed by surgery and a prescription for a narcotic pain medication.

This may be a topic you do not wish to include in your autobiography. Consider, however, that if you write about your experience, someone in a future generation might read your passage and glean some help from it. There might be just one segment of your story that resonates for someone reading it fifty years from now that might get them through a dark time.

- Is this a story about your struggle with addiction, or are you writing about a family member or friend?

- How did the exposure to the drug begin?

- What was the particular drug?

- How and when did you realize that the use of the drug had developed into an addiction?

- How did you or your family member/friend procure the drug when all legal avenues were no longer available? Where was the money coming from?

Write about the experiences you remember, including who was around to help, how long the addiction lasted, whether there was any attempt to go to a rehabilitation facility, and the present day condition of your own addiction or that of your family member/friend.

What consequences have occurred from your doing drugs or your drug addiction? What have you learned? What would you tell your great-grandchild or great-niece or nephew about what you have been through and how they could benefit from knowing about your experience? (See TOPIC 42: HEALTH and TOOL SHEET L: HEALTH RECORDS).

3: ADVICE

Advice is easily given. However, the human condition is that we are usually less willing to accept advice. What advice do you remember asking/getting from your family members, good friends, teachers, professionals, mentors, and books? What advice have you sought through the Internet or social media?

What kind of advice are/were you seeking? Did you seek those who would agree with you or those who might not, even if it meant hearing something you might not like? What was the value of their advice? What kind of advice have you found to be unhelpful? Did you change your course of action?

What advice do you have regarding raising children, parenting, or caring for elderly parents? What about advice relating to work and politics? Write about advice you have on any topic that comes to mind.

Some common topics for humans are love and hatred, forgiveness and blame; what advice do you have on these topics?

What is the best advice you have been given? Were you receptive to the advice straight away or not? Did you ever follow the good advice? Explain.

4: AFFIRMATIONS

Affirmations are a method to heal yourself. Affirmations are positive statements reversing negative messages you have received. Writing an affirmation is one of the first steps to personal inner healing. Think of a feeling or belief that keeps you from accessing your deepest "inner peace." Was it something you have been told like "You have a big nose"? In this example, you could write an affirmation such as "I am beautiful just the way I am!" Then read this two to three times a day. One idea is to put it on your bathroom mirror so it is visible. You can read your affirmations quietly, but they have more power if you read them aloud. You probably acquired your issue because you were *told or heard* something negative about you. Thus to *hear* the opposite belief helps create a new inner message to hear in your mind. To use a metaphor, it is like painting a wall. The old paint remains, but with affirmations—a new coat of paint—you no longer see the flaws on the wall.

Think about your insecurities and reverse them through using affirmations. Here is a list of some usual affirmations:

- I am beautiful inside and out.

- I am thoughtful.

- I am generous.

- I am an excellent listener.

- I am perfect just the way I am.

5: ANIMALS & CRITTERS—DOMESTIC & WILD

Write about the pets you/others have owned and/or loved. Describe them (See TOOL SHEET B: ANIMALS & CRITTERS).

Tell the stories you have regarding your experiences with animals: domestic pets, toys/stuffed, farm, and wild animals and critters.

In detail, write your memoirs about your pet or any living creature. What was the pet? How big was it? How did you acquire your pet(s)? What was its name, and how was this name chosen? Did you share it? Did you breed your pet, and were there offspring? Did you train your pet? If so, how and what did the pet learn? What were some of the vocabulary words you used for training commands? Did your pet win any prizes? Did your pet embarrass you?

Did you grow up on a farm? Do you have experiences from being on a farm? Who lived on the farm? Explain in detail what animals you have known and your relationship with each one.

Tell about your experiences with aquatic creatures. Did you ever have reptiles or amphibians as pets? Did you ever swim with dolphins or see whales out in the ocean? Have you been to an aquarium or animal preserve, and if so, with whom?

Tell about your experiences with wild animals. Did you go to zoos? Have you been to the circus? Do you know anyone who has worked with a circus? Have you ever gone on safari? Describe all your experiences in detail.

Tell about your favorite stuffed animals. What did they look like? What did you name them? Who gave them to you? Do you still have them?

Please include any photographs you have kept of your animals and critters.

6: ARTS

What is your definition of art? Is art important to you? What is your philosophy regarding the arts? (See TOOL SHEET A: ACTIVITIES, HOBBIES, INTERESTS, COLLECTIBLES, & SPORTS).

The world is all about art and music. The world is made of matter, which takes on shapes and colors and patterns. The sounds of all living creatures and instruments is music. Art is anything that has shape or form. Art is important. If you're skeptical of this idea, then imagine wearing the clothes of the next four people you meet. Imagine going and finding your car to be neon orange. Why would it matter? It is just a color, but clearly we place importance on colors and shapes and develop associations with things.

What constitutes "art" in your home today? How has your family perceived art? As a child, did you ever dream of becoming an artist? Are you an artist? What is your dream for your children relating to art?

What are your memories or feelings regarding the arts as they relate to the topics below? Please explain in detail. If you are an artist, please expound in your own style.

Below are some words to jog your memory regarding art.

- Actresses/Actors
- Animation
- Architecture
- Billboards/signs
- Books
- Bulletin Boards
- Cinema
- Crafts
- Dance
- Decorative Arts
- Design
- Drawings
- Fashion
- Fiber Arts
- Furniture
- Graffiti
- Industrial Design
- Installations
- Interior Design
- Magazines
- Media
- Movies
- Museums
- Music
- Operas
- Paintings
- Performing Arts
- Photography
- Plays
- Poems
- Print Making
- Prints
- Quotes
- Radio Programs
- Reliefs
- Sayings
- Sculptures
- Songs
- Television Programs
- Wall Hangings

What experiences in your daily life and in your travels have you had regarding museums, art galleries, lessons, personal collections, art history, and cultural art?

What works of art do you love and/or hate? Has a work of art ever changed your perspective or ideas about something?

Do you have a favorite period or style of art? What artists, living or deceased, have been most influential to you?

If you could have a conversation with any artist, living or deceased, who would it be, and what would you ask this artist? What would you like to say about how you feel about their accomplishments?

7: BALANCING LIFE

Imagine your life being on a disk balanced by one center point. How balanced is your life? (See Topic 48: INNER CHILD).

How well do you manage your life? Do you run your life or does it run you? We all have life stages, which dictate certain obligations, yet we do have many choices in how we address them. How conscientious are you about how you spend your time? Are you proactive or a procrastinator? How much passion is in your life?

There are many different parts of life: mental, physical, intellectual, and spiritual. Describe some present day obstacles. Are these obstacles ones you can control or not? Explain in detail.

BALANCING

Eating well	vs.	Eating poorly
Enjoying home life	vs.	Travel
Exercising regularly	vs.	Not exercising or not doing enough
Family	vs.	Time alone
Intellectual pursuits	vs.	Entertainment
Spending too much	vs.	Saving money
Work	vs.	Play/relaxing

Think about the amount of time you spend alone and regrouping, on the Internet, with others that nurture you, with others that need you, with others in a work environment, playing or having enjoyment/social time.

Does this exercise challenge you to alter your behavior or not? Explain.

8: BECOMING A ...

You can use these questions to explore your own childhood as well as those of your siblings, children, and other important people in your life. Try to recall what you were like at different stages in your life, either through direct memories, photographs, or family stories. Ask your mother and father, guardians, siblings, family, and best friends about how you changed over the years (See also TOPIC 10: BIRTH & COMING INTO THIS WORLD).

TODDLER YEARS

- What were your favorite toys, games, songs, sayings, foods, and friends? Include any growth charts.

- Include any memories that you have regarding siblings, secrets shared, special hiding places, friends, likes, dislikes, etc..

- How do you remember yourself as a child regarding looks, likes, dislikes, phobias, loves, and behaviors?

- Do you like your name? Have you ever wished it were different? Have you added to or changed your name? Have you ever been called by another name, or wished that you were? If so, what is the name and explain.

- Did you have any birthmarks? If yes, did they go away or not? Did they present any challenges for you?

CHILDHOOD

- What changes took place for you?

- What changes took place in your family, community, state, and world as you were growing up?

- What new conveniences, trends, etc., were introduced during these years?

- What plans and dreams did you have?

- What did you wish for? What did you receive and how meaningful was it? What did you not get that was disappointing?

- How did you begin to learn about becoming an adolescent and growing into maturity?

ADOLESCENCE

- What changes took place for you?

- What changes took place in your family, community, state, and world as you were growing up?

- What new conveniences, trends, etc., were introduced during these years?

- What plans and dreams did you have?

- What did you wish for? What did you receive and how meaningful was it? What did you not get that was disappointing?

ADULTHOOD

- What changes have taken place for you?

- What changes took place in your family, community, state, and the world?

- What modern conveniences, trends, etc., have come about?

- What plans and dreams did/do you have?

- What were/are your wishes?

- When did you leave home? Describe the day from the time you woke up to when you left, with all five or six senses.

- What did you take with you?

- What were the best and worst parts about leaving home?

- What were the easiest/hardest experiences you faced as a result of leaving home?

- What were the easiest/hardest experiences of being on your own?

RETIREMENT

- When did you retire? Describe the day with all five or six senses.

- If you have not retired, when are you planning to?

- What changes have taken place for you?

- What changes have taken place in your family, community, state, and world?

- What modern conveniences, trends, etc.?

- What plans did/do you have?

- What were/are your wishes?

- How well did you plan for your retirement? If you have not retired, how well are you planning for that day?

- What was the best part and worst part about retiring? What was the most unexpected awareness you discovered?

9: BELIEFS & RELIGION

As children, our beliefs were heavily influenced by what our parents/family and other people believed in. What beliefs or religious practices were you exposed to while growing up?

As we mature and hear of other beliefs, thoughts, and philosophies, we form our own beliefs. How have your beliefs evolved?

Important events from the loss of a loved one to rehabilitation can bring us closer to believing in a higher power. Explain in detail your experiences and beliefs.

EXTRASENSORY PERCEPTION (ESP)

Do you believe in ESP? Do you know anyone who believes in ESP? Explain the experiences you or someone you know has had regarding ESP.

GHOSTS & THE SUPERNATURAL

Some believe they have come in contact, directly or indirectly, with the supernatural. If you have, share your encounters. What have you heard firsthand from another regarding this? If you do not believe in the supernatural, please give the reasons why.

IMAGINARY FRIENDS

Often children have imaginary friends. Have you or anyone you have known had one? Explain.

METAPHYSICS[2]

What is your philosophy of being? What supernatural powers do you believe in? Do you believe in a "higher power"? Explain in detail.

PAST LIVES

Some people believe they have had past lives. Do you? Do you believe you will continue on, and if so, what do you think your next life or lives might be and why? What do you hope and why?

Have you been in a relationship with someone in this life who was in your past life? If so, who? What was your relationship with him/her in your past life? How did your past relationship and today's relationship intertwine? What did you learn from this relationship?

---

[2] Metaphysics: a division of philosophy that is concerned with the fundamental nature of reality and being and that includes ontology, cosmology, and often epistemology (Merriam-Webster).

RELIGION

What are your religious beliefs? Were you brought up practicing a certain faith or belief? Have you continued to practice the same religion? Why or why not?

Describe the religious culture in your home when growing up and now in present day. Have there been any family disagreements that were based on how you felt about religion?

What was your father's religion? Your mother's religion? Was there a religious ceremony performed when you were born to formalize your religious affiliation?

What were the dates of your religious events and festivities?

Were the schools you attended affiliated with a certain religion?

If you do not practice a certain religion, do you consider yourself a spiritual person? Describe your spiritual beliefs. Are you an atheist or an agnostic? Explain in detail.

Do you have godparents? If so, why were they chosen? What is their relationship to you and your parents, and where do they live now?

Who were the most influential people in your life regarding your religious upbringing?

Is it important to you to provide some religious education for your children?

How often do you take part in religious activities? Did/does your religion dictate a certain lifestyle, mode of dress, or diet? Describe in detail.

10: BIRTH & COMING INTO THIS WORLD

For the following questions answer first about your birth and then (if you have children) answer the same questions about your children's births.

- What do you know about the birth?

- Do you have a baby book or journals about the birth?

- Do you have any photos of the first few days of baby's life?

- Where did the birth take place—in a hospital, at home, or somewhere else?

- Who aided the delivery? A doctor, midwife, or family member?

- Were there any complications with the child's birth?

- Was the mother medicated, or was it a "natural" birth?

- Was the birth achieved by Cesarean section?

- Was the child born prematurely, on time, or late?

- If it was a premature birth, how long was the child kept in the hospital?

- How much did the child weigh?

- How long did the child measure?

- What time of day was the child born?

- Who was present at the child's birth?

- Did the child have any birthmarks? Where were they? Did they go away?

- What was the child's birth order in the family?

- What is the story behind choosing the child's name?

- Was the child breast-fed?

- Do you have health records from the child's infancy? (See TOOL SHEET L: HEALTH RECORDS).

- Who was the obstetrician? Who was the pediatrician?

- Was the child inoculated with the standard vaccines of the time? Explain.

- Was the child a colicky baby?

- Did the child have godparents? If yes, who were they? Were the godparents actively a part of the child's life?

- Was there a religious ceremony or celebration to welcome the child into the world?

- Was the child given any special baby gifts?

11: BOUNDARIES

A boundary within a personal relationship allows one to share only what one wants with another person. This can relate to the physical or emotional space you occupy, the amount of information you share with another, or physical possessions. Boundaries are usually considered a good thing to have in order for you to keep your personal space, have some privacy, and feel confident that you are not giving another more than you are able or want to.

The negative side to having boundaries is that if you shut yourself off from others, you may feel alone or isolated. You may alienate people without realizing what has happened. How would you describe your boundaries with others in general or with a particular person?

Boundaries can also exist within physical spaces, from sharing a room or an apartment to owning adjacent property and having neighbors.

Share your experiences and stories about boundaries.

What have you learned and how do you feel about creating or letting go of boundaries?

How do you establish boundaries while still being respectful with others?

12: CELEBRATIONS & FESTIVE TIMES

(See your CHRONOLOGICAL CALENDAR OF YOUR LIFE to help you remember where you were at each celebration. See TOPIC 22: DATES TO REMEMBER).

For each of the celebrations listed below, try to write as much information as you can remember.

- Who and what was the celebration for or about?

- The dates and ages of the people involved and your age at the time

- Who attended?

- What did you wear?

- What did others wear?

- Presents or gifts that were given

- Where was the venue? What was the atmosphere/theme?

- Who gave the party?

- Describe the food and beverages.

- Was champagne served?

- Was there a cake or special dessert?

- What traditions were performed?

- Any idea of the financial costs?

- What are your best and worst memories about this celebration?

Consider the following types of celebrations:

- Anniversaries
- Baptisms, christenings
- Birthdays
- Divorce
- Family celebrations—other
- Funerals and memorial services
- Graduations
- Parties in general
- Promotions
- Religious celebrations
- Reunions
- School celebrations
- Weddings

13: CHARITY

Charity is an act of kindness and can include offering your time or giving financially or through material goods. What have you done to help others? Was it done with their knowledge? How was it funded? Please explain in detail your charitable activities and how you spend your hours. What did you learn? What did you take away from the experience?

14: COLLECTIBLES

List the collections you have had.

How old were you when you started each collection?

How did the collection start?

Did someone else own the collection before it became yours?

What is the value of these collections monetarily and personally?

Are there any rare pieces in any of the collections? Do you have them insured?

If so, how did you decide on which company to use?

Have you made an inventory of your collections? Do you intend to leave these collections to certain individuals or donate them? (See TOOL SHEET A: ACTIVITIES, HOBBIES, INTERESTS, COLLECTIBLES, & SPORTS and TOOL SHEET M: INVENTORY).

15: COMES FROM

Here are some words that can act as prompts for you. Write down what first comes to mind. This is meant to be an explorative exercise.

Example: Intelligence comes from *genetics and a curious mind*

- Adventurousness comes from
- Affection comes from
- Aggressiveness comes from
- Artistic talent comes from
- Athleticism comes from
- Beauty comes from
- Boastfulness comes from
- Bossiness comes from
- Bravery comes from
- Broadmindedness comes from
- Clumsiness comes from
- Considerateness comes from
- Craziness comes from
- Creativity comes from
- Crying comes from
- Determination comes from
- Dependability comes from

- Dignity comes from
- Dishonesty comes from
- Drama comes from
- Eccentricity comes from
- Emotionlessness comes from
- Empathy comes from
- Energeticness comes from
- Enterprising comes from
- Falseness comes from
- Fashionable comes from
- Frustration comes from
- Generosity comes from
- Good natured comes from
- Goodness comes from
- Good memory comes from
- Gregariousness comes from
- Happiness comes from
- Hardworking comes from

- Healthiness comes from
- Honorable comes from
- Hotheaded comes from
- Imaginative comes from
- Indecisiveness comes from
- Independent comes from
- Indifference comes from
- Intuitiveness comes from
- Jealousy comes from
- Judgmentalness comes from
- Keen foresight comes from
- Kindness comes from
- Kindred spirits come from
- Laughing comes from
- Laziness comes from
- Long winded comes from
- Loving comes from
- Loyalty comes from
- Manipulativeness comes from
- Motivation comes from
- Naivety comes from
- Opinionated comes from
- Outspokenness comes from

- Patience comes from
- Peacefulness comes from
- Positive thinking comes from
- Pretty comes from
- Quick-mindedness comes from
- Relaxing comes from
- Reliability comes from
- Resourcefulness comes from
- Respectful comes from
- Romantic comes from.
- Shyness comes from
- Spirituality comes from
- Submissiveness comes from
- Sneakiness comes from
- Spontaneity comes from
- Tactfulness comes from
- Thoughtlessness comes from
- Tidiness comes from
- Trusting comes from
- Trustworthiness comes from
- Unaware comes from
- Unemotional comes from
- Unique comes from

- Vindictive comes from
- Visionary comes from
- Well-adjusted comes from

- Well-mannered comes from
- Workaholic comes from
- Young-minded comes from

16: CREATIVITY

Some of us are more creative than others. Creativity is an aptitude. Yet each of us has a creative side that is unique. Creativity may be illustrated by creating a material object, or it may be in thoughts used to write or in your manner of speaking. Some people, like musicians, are always hearing music in their heads, and creative thinkers are always having ideas flooding their minds, an endless stream of creativity that cannot be tamed. Do you have a mind that can relax easily, or do you find your mind is always creating new ideas and thoughts?

Tell about your talents and your creative side. Include your writings and artwork, or write about an activity where you feel your strongest creative side comes out and shines. This could be any activity such as gardening, cooking, dancing, acting, decorating, etc. (See TOPIC 6: ARTS and TOOL SHEET A: ACTIVITIES, HOBBIES, INTERESTS, COLLECTIBLES, & SPORTS).

17: CRIME—CIVIL & CRIMINAL

PART ONE

The topic of criminal activity and your family and acquaintances may not be relevant for many people. For those who have been exposed to criminal activity, either personally or because of other family members, or friends this topic may be very sensitive. Whether or not you choose to include your writing on this in your book is not the important part. It is more important that you write about it to understand how it influenced you in any way. Was there shame? Embarrassment? A family secret? Has anyone criticized you regarding this?

For some families, criminal involvement by a family member/acquaintance can have life-long consequences. It may be only short-lived. It could involve "white-collar" criminal activity. Many times, families choose to hide any criminal activity from others or try to move on from an unfortunate time in their lives. Sometimes, individuals turn their experience into a positive outcome by becoming an advocate or mentor for others who have been affected by similar circumstances.

Write about your experiences here; start from the beginning and tell the story of what happened. Who was involved? What was the nature of the crime? Was it a "victimless" crime or were people hurt? What specifically happened? Was the crime reported or found out?

Was there an arrest and ensuing criminal/civil trial? Was there a sentence imposed? Was jail time served? Was there a fine or monetary restitution?

If the criminal activity did not result in an arrest or any legal consequences, you might want to write about the personal consequences that have resulted. Has there been a change in outlook for you or your family member? Describe what has occurred. Did you experience remorse, regret, or lessons learned? Or did the experience have little or no effect on future behavior?

What would you do for others who are exposed to criminal activity?

PART TWO

Have you or a family member or acquaintance been the victim of a crime? What was the nature of the crime? Was the perpetrator caught? What was the outcome?

Have you or your family members and acquaintances needed to seek help to recover from the experience? Have there been any life-long consequences? Are you able to speak about what happened, or do you prefer people not to know?

If someone you care deeply for has been the victim of a crime, how were you supportive? What has it meant for you that a loved one has been harmed by or harmed others in a criminal act? How do you cope with your experience? Could your relationship with this person sustain itself?

18: CROSSROADS

In life there are passages or places we choose and others that force us to change our lives. Coming to crossroad is to choose a path. There are times when we have a plan and the road is visible, but sometimes circumstances are beyond our control and we need to take a different path. It demands that we stop and look hard at what happened and what choices are available.

- What challenges did you have to accept?

- How did you deal with them, and was it with integrity and wisdom?

- More important, what did you learn?

You may choose to write about, paint, or draw a picture of this time in your life. It is freeing. Keep in mind the purpose of the process is not to see the result of the final product but for the experience—let it come out.

19: CURIOUS QUESTIONS

Over time, we encounter some very curious questions. Sometimes they are questions posed by a child that are amusing to adults. Sometimes there are questions that are too personal and it takes us a long time to muster the nerve to ask. Sometimes we just know something intuitively and want verification. (Names may be omitted here).

- What are your earliest memories?

- What do you want to ask your family members about their lives?

- What do you want to ask your friends about their lives?

- What are the biggest blocks in your life to real happiness?

- What if you had different siblings?

- What if you had to change places with another person you know well, who would it be?

- What if you could be anyone else, who would you be?

- What if you could have an adventure and be guaranteed not to get hurt, what would you love to do?

- What if you had only one year to live, how would you spend it?

- What if you could have a pet at no cost or inconvenience, what would it be?

- What would a day in your life be like if you woke up as the opposite sex?

- What if your finances were unlimited? Would you change your life? If so, in what ways?

- What if you could change one characteristic of your personality, what would it be?

- What natural talent do you wish you had?

- What if you could alter any part(s) of your body, what would it be?

- What if you won $10,000,000 in the lottery, what would you do with it?

20: CURRENT EVENTS

How active are you in staying current with the news? By what methods do you get the news? Do you obtain your news from a certain political perspective?

Do you feel the news media have political statements to make in their reporting?

What has been the most startling news headline you can remember? Where were you at the time? How did you react to such news? Explain in detail.

Consider these events and write what you can remember:

- Wars: the World Wars, the Cold War, Korea, Vietnam, the War on Drugs, Desert Storm, Afghanistan, Iraq, the War on Terror

- Assassinations: President Kennedy, Dr. Martin Luther King, Jr., Robert Kennedy, John Lennon

- The 9/11/2001 attacks in the USA; the aftermath/reaction to the attacks

- Major legal decisions/changes: Brown v. Board of Education (desegregation of schools/bussing), the Civil Rights Act, the Voting Rights Act, the Equal Rights Amendment (never passed), Roe v. Wade (abortion in the USA), same-sex marriage, opening of the military to gay service members, medical and/or recreational marijuana, physician-assisted suicide

- Mention other momentous events that were important to you.

21: CUT & PASTE

MATERIAL FROM PUBLIC SOURCES

Research and download any news from the Internet that has been posted about you, your family, community, safety, politics, world events, prices of that time, etc. that you regard worth having. Remember to record the date and from which source you downloaded the information in order to give proper attribution. Go to your town clerk's office, and get copies of deeds and other papers regarding your properties.

NEWSPAPER CLIPPINGS

Include scanned copies of the newspaper clippings that you regard worth having which are about you, your family and/or friends, community, safety, politics, world events, prices of a time period (you can order a newspaper of the day you were born. What will these clippings tell about the time when you lived?

OBITUARY NOTICES

Find and either download or make copies of obituary notices of family, friends, and individuals whose lives meant a great deal, perhaps a politician or an author.

PHOTOGRAPHS

Do you have photographs? It is important to identify the photo by where it was taken, when it was taken, who is in the photo, and the significance of their relationship to you. State here where your photographs, movies, videos, and negatives are kept.

SCRAPBOOKS & PHOTO ALBUMS

If you have any scrapbooks of your childhood or family members, scan them and make these also into a book. At least make copies and put them into a notebook for future generations to see.

Do you have any of the following?

- Art
- Awards
- Catalogs
- Certificates
- Charts
- Contracts
- Diaries
- Documents
- Drawings
- Letters
- Lists
- Loans
- Magazines

- Maps
- Newspapers
- Notes
- Pictures
- Play programs
- Questions
- Quotes
- Records
- Reports
- Souvenirs
- Sports events flyers
- Tests
- Trophies

22: DATES TO REMEMBER

Record the dates of important events and milestones: becoming of legal age, historical events, family celebrations, birthdays, marriages, draft notices, meeting a President, trips, the World's Fair, the first automobile you bought, etc.

On your LIFE CALENDAR, or on a standard monthly calendar, list the annual dates of special events for those to whom you feel especially close to and/or are related:

- Anniversaries
- Birthdays
- Deaths
- Weddings

January

1	10	19
2	11	20
3	12	21
4	13	22
5	14	23
6	15	24
7	16	25
8	17	26
9	18	27

28	30	
29	31	

February

1	11	21
2	12	22
3	13	23
4	14	24
5	15	25
6	16	26
7	17	27
8	18	28
9	19	29
10	20	

March

1	9	17
2	10	18
3	11	19
4	12	20
5	13	21
6	14	22
7	15	23
8	16	24

25	28	31
26	29	
27	30	

April

1	11	21
2	12	22
3	13	23
4	14	24
5	15	25
6	16	26
7	17	27
8	18	28
9	19	29
10	20	30

May

1	8	15
2	9	16
3	10	17
4	11	18
5	12	19
6	13	20
7	14	21

22	26	30
23	27	31
24	28	
25	29	

June

1	11	21
2	12	22
3	13	23
4	14	24
5	15	25
6	16	26
7	17	27
8	18	28
9	19	29
10	20	30

July

1	7	13
2	8	14
3	9	15
4	10	16
5	11	17
6	12	18

19	24	29
20	25	30
21	26	31
22	27	
23	28	

August

1	12	23
2	13	24
3	14	25
4	15	26
5	16	27
6	17	28
7	18	29
8	19	30
9	20	31
10	21	
11	22	

September

1	5	9
2	6	10
3	7	11
4	8	12

13	19	25
14	20	26
15	21	27
16	22	28
17	23	29
18	24	30

October

1	12	23
2	13	24
3	14	25
4	15	26
5	16	27
6	17	28
7	18	29
8	19	30
9	20	31
10	21	
11	22	

November

1	4	7
2	5	8
3	6	9

10	17	24
11	18	25
12	19	26
13	20	27
14	21	28
15	22	29
16	23	30

December

	11	22
1	12	23
2	13	24
3	14	25
4	15	26
5	16	27
6	17	28
7	18	29
8	19	30
9	20	31
10	21	

23: DEATH

Explain what experiences you have had with death. Explain your attitude/perception regarding death. This can be about the death of a person or an animal.

- How have you handled your experiences with death?
- What advice do you have about dealing with death?
- Do you have fears about death? If so, what are they?
- What deaths of national or international figures have you experienced? What was the public's reaction? Your reaction?

When someone passes, some communicate with him or her. There may be times that you feel the person is with you. Often people feel the deceased person can see them. How did you create an understanding of what those who have passed can hear, see, and know of what we do? Explain how this relates to those you have lost.

YOURSELF

- Do you have a signed will and trust?
- Where are your legal documents located?
- What preparations have you taken for when you pass away, if suddenly/unexpectedly?
- If you knew you had a limited time to live, what would you do differently?
- Do you believe you have had past lives? Do you believe you will have future lives?
- Have you written an epitaph?

- Have you written your obituary?

- Are your executors still the correct individuals? Do you have enough executors in line of preference?

- Have you written your living will?

- Do you have in your addresses a section on who should be contacted when you do pass?

- Have you written your statement of wishes in case you are alive but unable to make decisions and how you want to be cared for (from location to foods and clothing you wish to have) and what material objects you want with you during this time?

- Have you written a formal advance directive that spells out your instructions on whether you want to be kept alive on life support or allowed to die if you go into a coma or become "braindead"?

- Have you made plans for your virtual assets like phone accounts or social media? It is important that your cell phone is not cut off because for many of us it is the access to all our accounts to get new passwords. Your family/executor would need your cell password.

- Have you created an email for another Remembering(their name)@.... for people to send photos, memoirs, and videos to, in order to create a book and movie?

24: DECADE DECALS

What have been your most important accomplishments over the past decades of your life? Note the year and your age, then explain the "who, what, why, where," and any other details you would like to include.

What do you hope to accomplish in each of your next decades? Explain what, why, where, your age, and the year.

- Ages 0–9

- Ages 10–19

- Ages 20–29

- Ages 30–39

- Ages 40–49

- Ages 50–59

- Ages 60–69

- Ages 70–79

- Ages 80–89

- Ages 90–99

- Ages 100+

25: DIFFICULT TIMES

ABUSE

Unfortunately, statistics show that many individuals are abused physically, emotionally, and financially. Although you may wish this topic of abuse to be forgotten, it is so important that it be addressed. This is the person you have come to be and that developed the strength it took to endure and survive.

Only you can make the decision whether or not to include your experiences in your autobiography, but I truly encourage everyone to face their ghostly enemies, if not the enemies themselves. I feel it is only by sharing what you have been through that you will come to realize there are so many others out there who have had similar experiences. You can find support; you are not alone.

List the situations where abuse was threatened or implemented. Name each of the individuals (you may choose to use fictitious names); include dates, your age, and what was done about it if anything. What have you come to understand about your experience? You may choose not to include this section in your finished autobiography. Some situations need time, maturity, and distance to understand, to accept, and to forgive.

ALCOHOL & OTHER ADDICTIVE SUBSTANCES

For many of us, alcohol and other addictive substances have been a part of our lives. Please tell about your experiences in any form, from drinking, to being around alcoholics and addicts, to being in possession of an illegal substance. A "dry drunk" is a person who is no longer drinking but who has never worked through their issues. This person can be as difficult as an active alcoholic. (See TOPIC 2: ADDICTIONS & SUBSTANCE ABUSE).

Describe any experiences regarding substance abuse, from prescription medications to illegal drugs. What have you learned, especially with your loved ones? Did anyone go to a rehabilitation program? Was this productive or not? Explain why.

BULLYING

List your most difficult memories if you have been bullied. Explain how, when, and where. How old were you and what were your feelings about each situation then and now? Have you shared these memories with anyone? What did you learn from this experience? How can others benefit from what you have learned?

Were you ever on the giving end of bullying or complicit in another's bullying? If so, why did you bully others? How did you feel about it then and now? Did you ever address it with those you bullied?

DANGEROUS SITUATIONS

Have you ever felt that you were in a truly dangerous situation? How quickly did you realize your circumstances had become dangerous? Were you alone, or were there people around to help? Describe what happened. What did you do to alleviate this situation? What was the outcome?

DIVORCE

Life is difficult enough without having to experience a divorce. This is one of the most devastating moments in life I believe, even if you know it is the right step to take. Divorce is about changing your entire life, not just about getting rid of a person.

Everyone is affected by divorce—your family, children, friends, and even pets. Do you feel that you were treated differently because of your gender? Do you feel that you were unfairly judged, ostracized, or that you lost friends after you were divorced? How did you navigate this time in your life? Did you find support through therapy or other means?

- Have your beliefs about divorce changed over time?

- How have you changed after experiencing your own divorce or those of others close to you?

- What do you think is the main reason why there are so many divorces?

- What were the hardships for your family and your children?

- What were your thoughts about improving the process of divorce?

- What were the benefits of your own divorce for you and others?

- Most importantly, what was learned from the experience?

- Have you considered divorce, but never gone through with it? What are your thoughts about this?

- Do you have any regrets after becoming divorced? Do you wish you had gotten one and did not? Do you feel that you would have done it differently?

MORE

Difficult times are, of course, not restricted to the topics given above (See TOPIC 17: CRIME—CIVIL & CRIMINAL). You could also choose one of the topics below to write about:

- Embarrassments
- Health crises
- Legal issues
- Losses
- Parents' remarriage
- Sexual assault
- Tragedies
- Unjustified Experiences

26: DNA

What physical traits run through your family? What have you inherited?

Some of the genetic traits are as follows:

- Aptitudes
- Athletic ability
- Health: good and bad
- Intelligence
- Learning disability

- Personality
- Physical coloring of skin, eyes, and hair
- Voice or laughter
- Your body shape

We are born with physical characteristics that we inherited from our biological parents. We can change some of these to an extent, but our basic physical selves and certain features are uniquely ours.

Tell how you feel or have felt about your body.

- What do you like or dislike the most about your physical self?
- What traits do you know run in your family that you do not see in yourself?
- If you were adopted, have you tried to find your biological family?
- Do you have photographs of your ancestors that resemble photographs of yourself?

27: DREAMS & NIGHTMARES

Dreams are thoughts, feelings, and visions we see when resting or sleeping. They might be about something you truly want to have happen in your life. A dream might be a vision you created from your imagination, like a determination to conquer all obstacles in your way.

A nightmare brings disturbing thoughts that can make perfect sense or not be reasonable at all. Have you had a reoccurring dream? Do you believe that your diet, exercise, medications, or lack thereof have anything to do with them? Did you have nightmares that you cannot explain?

Have you written your dreams and nightmares down right away? What do you feel is the symbolism of these dreams, the meanings they hold? When you have nightmares, what are the fears and conflicts that cause these fears?

Please write about your nightmares with as much detail as you can. It may not make sense, but still write it down. Writing them down may help you remember and draw insights from your nightmares.

28: EDUCATION

Gaining an education is the process of learning and developing knowledge, skills, and training. We acquire education from attending an educational institution, being taught, through reading or conducting research, and from life experiences.

Please write about the education you have received and accomplished. Have you used your education as you planned, or did you do something different?

Please share your stories regarding the following (See TOOL SHEET G: EDUCATION):

- Awards
- Books
- Classrooms
- Clubs
- Homeschooling
- Lessons
- Online classes
- Plays

- Quality of your education
- Report cards
- Sports at educational institutions
- Subjects you chose
- Teachers
- Teaching
- Workshops

29: ENVIRONMENT & REAL ESTATE

PERSONAL ENVIRONMENT

Describe your various homes from birth to present day. Did you live in houses, apartments, boats, tents, or trailers? What was your "home" like?

For each of your homes, give a physical description and geographical location (See TOOL SHEETS I: ENVIRONMENT, J: FAMILY HISTORY, and T: REAL ESTATE).

Explain who your neighbors were and your family's relationship to them.

How close were other family members to your home? Who were the significant people in your life in the home?

Describe your room color, décor, and size. Did you have to share it? What was the furniture like? Did you have to keep your room clean, or were you allowed to leave it as you wished?

Describe the individual rooms of your house. What were some of the happy and unhappy moments related to these rooms? Did you create special rooms or spaces outside for yourself, such as workrooms, studios, quiet spaces, music rooms, gardens, etc?

YOUR TOWN/CITY/COMMUNITY

Describe the different communities where you have lived. Include physical descriptions as well as the climate and weather.

- What were the neighborhoods like?

- What were the approximate populations and demographics of each one?

- What were the major industries and commerce?

- What schools did you attend? Were there any other schools nearby?

- Were there opportunities to participate in civic activities? Was there a sense of community?

- Were you part of a faith community?

WORLD ENVIRONMENT

How do you perceive your personal relationship with the greater world environment?

What do you do to help preserve the Earth from the damage that has been caused by humans?

What are some of the current things people can do to help the world's condition? How much are you willing to give up to contribute?

What do you think the future of the world environment will look like in 25, 50, or 100 years from now? Record the year that you are writing your thoughts.

Have you experienced a natural disaster, earthquake, etc?

30: EPITAPH

Write an appropriate epitaph for yourself. Ask some close friends what they would write for you. You can, of course, edit these or delete them if you choose. You can also mention epitaphs you have read and liked.

31: ESSENCE OF YOU

What is your essence? Who are you within your own mind, the one you do not always project? What characteristics do you have? How have you become the person you are today?

Where does your sense of morality, integrity, respect, and trust come from? Do you live by high morals, or do you struggle with decision-making and sometimes lose your way? Do you see things clearly, or are you apt to question most situations due to uncertainty?

What do you use as guidelines for your behaviors? What rules and guidelines do you think are helpful to keep in mind as you go through life?

How much do you buy into the consumer marketing regarding all you should be? How do you deal with the pressures of society? (See TOPIC 48: INNER CHILD and TOOL SHEET D: CHARACTERISTICS).

32: FANTASY

We often imagine life as it could be or wish it could be. From our early childhood, stories take us to many imaginary places with imaginary creatures. The human mind is creative—do you find yourself to be more creative with guidelines or when you work without boundaries to your thinking?

Share your wildest dreams and fantasies—visual, meditative, cognitive, or imaginative. Consider wealth, fame, travel, and relationships.

If you could have designed your life from the start with the hindsight you have now, how would it look in detail? Is it different from how it has been?

If you were to come back as a superhero, who would you be?

What are your favorite stories, movies, and books about fantasy? Who are your favorite characters? Favorite movie scenes? What character do you wish you could be and in what movie?

33: FASHION & MANNERS

FASHION

The popular modes of clothes, jewelry, shoes, hem-lengths, and formal versus casual wear have changed many times over the years. Explain how fashion is or is not important to you and in what ways. Fashion is a broad scope of what is thought to be acceptable and "hip" for a certain time period, but inevitably fades away to make room for newer trends. Sometimes, fashion repeats itself and certain styles become popular once again. Share some of your memories of your grandparents, parents, and other family members and how they appeared. Have you saved any garments or accessories from their wardrobes?

Gather your old family photographs and write about how you felt about your fashion then. Describe some of the clothing that you wore growing up. What did you like to wear? Did your parents allow you to pick out your own clothes at the store, or at home in the morning? How did you feel about this?

What were the popular hairstyles for both men and women over your lifetime? Were any considered controversial? Why? Were there any dress codes in effect at your school or elsewhere? Have you ever had to wear a uniform?

Was there a particular decade of fashion you felt strongly about? Describe why.

Look online at the popular fashion trends from the year you were born and comment on the images. Look at magazine covers and old movies and notice how different things are now.

MANNERS

Manners reflect very particular cultural preferences, influenced by place and time. What is proper in one country is not at all acceptable in another. Over the years manners within some cultures have changed and in others not at all. What manners were you taught? What manners do you have now? Explain your beliefs and behaviors.

34: FAVORITES

Beside each word, add your "favorite" for that particular word. If you have a strong reaction to a word, jot a note beside it. For example, "Tattoo." Most people have a strong opinion. Write your opinion down here. This is all about inspiring you to write.

- Airline
- Agriculture show
- Animal (domestic)
- Animal (wild)
- Appliance
- Architecture
- Art genre
- Artist
- Athlete
- Atmosphere
- Aunt
- Author
- Automobile
- Ballet
- Baseball team
- Basketball team
- Bedroom

- Bedtime story
- Bird
- Birthday
- Blue jeans
- Boat
- Book
- Book – autobiography
- Book – bought a signed book
- Book – novel
- Book – spiritual
- Boots
- Boxer
- Breakfast
- Bridge
- Building
- Candy

- Car
- Car ride
- Cat
- Charity
- Chewing gum
- Christmas
- Christmas tree
- Church
- City – American
- City – Canadian
- City – Foreign
- Clothing store
- Club
- Coffee
- Collectable
- Cologne
- Color
- Color – bedroom
- Color – clothing
- Color – eyes
- Color – hair
- Color – house
- Color – shoes
- Comedian

- Comic strip
- Commentator
- Cookbook
- Country to travel to
- Cousin
- Dances
- Day of the year
- Deodorant
- Department store – budget
- Department store – upscale
- Dessert
- Dinner
- Dog
- Dress
- Drink – alcoholic
- Drink – fruit
- Drink – non-alcoholic
- Drink – soda
- Entertainer
- Environment
- Farm animal
- Favorite place to visit with children
- Figure skater

- Film actor
- Film actress
- First lady
- Flower
- Food
- Football team
- Fox hunt
- Friend – female
- Friend – male
- Fruit
- Furniture
- Game to play
- Gifts to give
- Gifts to receive
- Grace you learned to say
- Grandparent
- Graduation you attended
- Greeting card
- Grocery store
- Halloween
- Hardware tools
- Headache remedy
- Hero
- Heroine

- Hobby
- Holiday
- Home
- Hotel – American
- Hotel – foreign
- Ice cream – brand and flavor
- Ice hockey team
- Interest
- Interior decorating
- Joke
- Journalist
- July 4th
- Kaleidoscopes
- Kiss
- Lover
- Lumber materials
- Lunch
- Magazine
- Meat
- Melody
- Memory
- Month
- Motorcycle

- Movie
- Museum
- Music
- Musical instrument
- Musician
- Myth
- Nanny/baby sitter
- New Year's Eve
- New Year's resolution
- Opera
- Orchestra
- Organization
- Outfit
- Painter/illustrator/sculptor
- Painting
- Participating sport
- Perfume
- Philosopher
- Photographs
- Place to be alone
- Place to be with family
- Place to be with lover
- Place to visit
- Plays

- Poem you memorized
- Political figure
- Port
- Prayer you memorized
- Pretend friend
- President of the United States
- Professor
- Purchase
- Quality in a friend
- Queen
- Quote
- Racehorse
- Radio program
- Recipe
- Relative
- Restaurant
- Royal person
- Saying
- Scent
- School
- Scripture
- Sculpture
- Season

- Shopping center
- Sibling
- Singer
- Skier
- Skiing mountain
- Sneaker
- Soccer team
- Song
- Sound
- Spectator sport
- Sport
- State
- Stock you owned
- Store
- Story
- Style of clothing
- Style of furniture
- Style of hair
- Style of house
- Subject
- Summer
- Step-relatives
- Swimmer
- Swimming spot

- Symphony
- Taste
- Tattoo
- Tea
- Teacher
- Television you owned
- Tennis court
- Tennis player
- Thanksgiving
- Time of day
- Toothbrush
- Train
- TV actor
- TV actress
- TV game show
- TV soap opera
- TV show
- Umbrella
- Uncle
- Vacation place for family
- Vacation place for one
- Vacation place for two
- Valentine's Day
- Vegetable

- Waterfall
- World leader
- Year in college
- Year in life

- Year in school
- Yogurt
- Zoo

35: FEAR & SHAME

What fears and shame have you experienced throughout your life that you feel have affected the quality of your life?

FEARS

- Fears can be about driving in heavy traffic, thinking or knowing a snake might be under your front steps, sleeping in total darkness, or a real life-threatening event.

- Where do you think these fears come from?

- What are some of your biggest fears?

- How do you overcome your fears?

- What were some fears you had as a child?

- What methods did/do you employ to cope with realistic fears, whether they are physical, financial, fear for others, health, death, being alone, growing old, fear of someone in particular, fear of failure, being unpopular, religious fears, or fears about the future?

SHAME

- Where does shame come from?

- How does one face his or her shame?

- How do you release your shame?

- How do you live with your shame?

36: FESTIVE TIMES & HOLIDAYS

What holidays are or have been special? How and why? Where did/do you go for the holidays? Who was with you? Describe the experience. What traditions were upheld? Which traditions do you continue, and which ones have you created? If you celebrate ones not listed here, please add them.

Ash Wednesday

Black Friday

Chinese New Year

Christmas Day

Christmas Eve

Columbus Day

Cyber Monday

Easter

Epiphany

Father's Day

First day of autumn

First day of spring

First day of summer

First day of winter

Flag Day

Good Friday

Grandparents' Day

Groundhog Day

Halloween

Hanukkah

Inauguration Day

Independence Day

Kwanzaa

Labor Day

Last Day of Chanukah

Lincoln's Birthday

Mardi Gras

Martin Luther King Day/Civil

Rights Day

Memorial Day

Mother's Day	Rodeo Day
National Freedom Day	Rosh Hashanah
National Wear Red Day	St. David's Day
Native American Day	St. Nicholas' Day
New Year's Day	St. Patrick's Day
New Year's Eve	State Holidays
Orthodox Christmas Day	Thanksgiving
Palm Sunday	US National Guard Birthday
Passover—First Day	Valentine's Day
Passover—Eighth Day	Veterans Day
Pearl Harbor Day	Washington's Birthday
Presidents Day	Winter Solstice

See more holidays at http://www.timeanddate.com/holidays/us/2017

37: FINANCIAL FACTS & KNOWLEDGE

What is your philosophy regarding your financial matters? What are your thoughts concerning these issues? (See TOPIC 47: INHERITANCE).

- Attorneys
- Banks
- Business affiliations
- Charge accounts
- Credit cards
- Finances
- Gambling
- Gifts
- Income tax, state tax
- Inheritance

- Insurance
- IRA accounts
- Leasing, credit cards
- Mutual bonds
- Pensions
- Rental
- Social Security
- Trusts, stocks
- Unemployment taxes
- Worker's compensation

- What is your philosophy regarding the budgets of the town/city you live in, your state, or your country?

- How did you learn about money growing up? Did you have an allowance? Did you have to do chores to earn your allowance? What was your first significant purchase?

- Explain the ways you have earned money throughout your life.

- How would you describe and explain the difference between a want and a need?

- What loans have you had or do you have? What is your philosophy regarding paying them off?

- Have you ever been in significant debt? What have you done to lower your debt?

- What responsibilities come with earning and saving money?

- Were you ever given money as a gift? Explain in detail.

- What financial windfalls or crises have you experienced?

- Were you taught to donate money, i.e. UNICEF boxes, church collections, raising money through group activities?

- Have you been able to save money as an adult? Do you have retirement savings?

- Do you make charitable donations?

- Have you ever been really jealous of another person because he or she has been financially able to have what you cannot afford? Do you know this person personally? If yes, how has this affected your relationship with that person?

- Have you ever written any articles about finances?

What are your approximate costs of living during any given year? Break them down into categories by kind such as needs/wants, and as compared to last year.

- Allowance
- Animals
- Art
- Children
- Clothes
- Collectibles
- Donations
- Education

- Employees
- Entertainment
- Equipment and appliances
- Family members
- Finances
- Food
- Gambling
- Games

- Gifts
- Hobbies
- Holidays
- Home utilities
- Insurance – all coverage policies
- Jewelry
- Legal expenses
- Maintenance
- Medical
- Mortgage/Rent
- Needs not mentioned
- Pets/Animals
- Presents
- Recreation
- Repairs
- Second home
- Sports
- Taxes
- Toys
- Utilities
- Vacations
- Vehicles
- Wants and desires

38: FIRSTS

Jot your answer down beside the word then return to explain in detail your experiences.

WHAT WAS YOUR FIRST ...

- Accident you were involved in
- Accident you witnessed
- Actress/Actor you met
- Advanced education
- Airline voyage
- Agriculture show you attended/showed in
- Animal experience (domestic)
- Animal experience (wild)
- Animal you had as a pet
- Appliance you bought/owned
- Asian restaurant
- Athletic event you won or was memorable
- Author you met
- Baby doll and her name
- Babysitting job you had
- Ballet you attended
- Bank/Savings account

- Baseball game you attended
- Basketball game you attended
- Bedroom you had, or had alone
- Bicycle
- Breathing machine
- Camera
- Camping trip
- Candy – (your first favorite candy)
- Car
- Cat
- Cell phone
- Charity to which you made a donation
- Choir song you sang
- Church Baptism and Confirmation
- City you visited (American)
- City you visited (Canadian)
- City you visited (foreign)
- Club to which you belonged
- Collection you started
- Cologne or perfume you wore
- Computer or other high-tech device
- Cookbook you loved
- Country you visited outside your home country
- Dance class

- Date

- Death you experienced

- Decorated your home/apartment

- Deodorant you bought

- Dessert you made

- Drink you made

- Dinner that totally failed

- Dinner you made that was a great success

- Dog

- Donkey basketball game you attended

- Dress you loved/still have

- Drink – alcoholic

- Drink – non-alcoholic

- Driver's license

- Embarrassment or best story of being ...

- Entertainer you met in person or went to see

- Famous person you met

- Farm experience

- Film actor – the first one you loved

- First lady you admired

- Flowers that were given to you

- Football game you went to see live

- Fox hunt you rode in

- Friend – female best friend

- Friend – male best friend

- Funny memory

- Furniture that you purchased

- Graduation

- Grandchild

- Gun you shot

- Halloween pumpkin you carved

- Hardware tools you purchased

- Hero you admired

- Hobby that you started

- Holiday

- Home you bought

- Home you rented

- Horse race you attended/you bet on

- Ice hockey team you watched live

- Illness that was serious

- Infatuation

- Injury

- Instrument you played or owned

- Job

- Joke you told

- Kaleidoscope you owned/made

- Kiss

- Lawn mower

- Lottery ticket purchased

- Lottery ticket that won

- Lover you had

- Magazine subscription you ordered

- Major birthday

- Membership you had

- Motorcycle

- Movie

- Museum you visited

- Mushroom you ate

- Music CD you bought

- Musical instrument you learned to play

- Musician you saw live in concert

- Nephew or niece

- New Year's Eve party you attended

- Ocean (your first time touching different oceans)

- Opera you attended

- Orchestra you attended

- Organization you started

- Painter/illustrator/sculpture you admired

- Painting you fell in love with

- Perfume you bought or received as a gift

- Pet

- Philosopher you believe and admire

- Photo camera you ever shot/picture you developed

- Photos you ever took/picture you developed

- Piano recital

- Play you were in

- Poem you memorized

- Poem you wrote and loved

- Political election

- Political figure you admired

- Professional haircut you had

- Professional photograph you had taken

- Purchase over a thousand dollars

- Purchases with your earned or saved money

- Raffle ticket you bought

- Raffle you won

- Radio program you listened to

- Recipe you fell in love with

- Restaurant where you had an embarrassing moment

- Romance

- Royal person you ever met

- School you attended

- Scripture you memorized

- Sculpture you made

- Sewing item you made

- Sewing machine you had

- Sexual encounter
- Shopping center you went to
- Shots you received to travel abroad
- Singer you saw live in concert
- Singing in public you did (caroling?)
- Skiing mountain you visited
- Skis you owned
- Sneakers you owned/you wore out
- Soccer game you attended/team you cheered
- Song you associated with a love
- Song you learned to play
- Sound you made on a musical instrument
- Spectator sport you went to
- Sport you participated in
- Stage performance
- Stepparent (you became or had)
- Step relatives
- Stock you bought
- Store you disliked and never returned to
- Story made up about you that hurt your feelings
- Stuffed animal
- Style of clothing you fell in love with
- Style of furniture you admired
- Subject you loved at school

- Surprise party for you
- Surprise party given by you
- Swimming sport you competed in
- Symphony you saw live
- Teacher
- Tennis court you played on
- Thanksgiving prayer you learned
- Train ride
- Traveling experience
- Tricycle
- TV actor you adored
- TV actress you adored
- TV game show you loved
- TV soap opera you loved
- Umbrella
- Vacation for family
- Vacation for one
- Vacation for two
- Valentine's Day when you got flowers
- Vegetable you were hesitant to eat
- Volunteer job
- Wagon
- Waterfall you made a wish on
- Winnings from a raffle

- World leader you voted for

- X-Ray

- Year of college

- Zoo you visited

39: FOODS & DRINKS

Food and drinks are a huge part of a person's life.

- What is the amount of time in an average week you spend on food? The purchasing, preparing, eating? What parts of a normal day are occupied with food?

- Write the cost of foods and keep receipts over the next few years. Note the price changes.

- What are some of your favorite foods?

- What is your relationship with foods? Are you an adventurous or a picky eater?

- Are you into heavy or healthy eating habits? Are you a vegetarian or vegan, or do you follow any specific diet?

- Have you grown to like certain foods that you did not like in your past?

- Have you been allergic to some foods? If yes, have your allergies gone away?

- Do you like to prepare food?

- Do you have favorite foods? Is it their flavor, texture, or fragrance you love? Memories of a past event?

- Do you "live to eat" or "eat to live"?

- What are some of your favorite cookbooks? Recipes?

- What are your favorite restaurants?

- If you have children, did you buy over-the-counter baby foods, or did you make your baby's foods?

- Do you enjoy cooking? Do you buy prepared foods?

- Do you have a favorite ethnic food?

- Do you cook similar foods that you had as a child, or have you changed the pattern?

- Food is a huge part of our social life. What stories do you remember about some of your gatherings?

- What is your ethnic background? Does this affect your food choices?

- Are there religious beliefs that affect how and what you eat?

- If you were about to have a birthday dinner with a personal chef all paid for, what would the menu be for the following: cocktail, appetizer, soup, bread, entrée, dessert, after dinner drink? Who would you invite?

What thoughts and stories do the following words inspire?

- AA (Alcoholics Anonymous)
- A la carte
- Alcoholic beverages
- Allergies
- Appetizers
- Baby feeding
- Banana
- Barbecue
- Batter
- Being polite at all costs
- Belching
- Best food presentation
- Binges
- Birthday parties
- Blackened
- Boating
- Brunch
- Buffet
- Burned food
- Burping
- Butlers
- Café events
- Camping over the fire
- Candies
- Canned foods
- Carvings
- Celebrations
- Chefs
- Children stories
- China
- Compliments
- Cookbook
- Cooking failures
- Cooking success
- Coolers
- Cost
- Cravings
- Dad's cooking
- Dehydrated
- Desserts
- Diets
- Donuts

- Drink
- Dump stories
- DWI
- Eating habits
- Eating in the car
- Embarrassing moments around food
- Ethnic Foods
- Exotic atmosphere
- Exotic foods
- Family traditions
- Fast foods
- Favorite chefs
- Favorite meal
- Favorite restaurant
- Food poisoning
- Food while driving
- Foods found in the wild
- Foods you hate
- Fowl
- Fragrances
- Freezer broken/without power
- Freezer surprises
- Friend's parents' cooking

- Frozen prepared food
- Fruit
- Frying
- Funniest meals
- Garbage bag failures
- Garnishes
- Grandparent's house
- Hangover
- Happy hour
- Health stores
- Holiday meals
- Homemade food
- Ice cream
- Insults
- Juices
- Junk food
- Longest meals ever
- Loveliest outdoor setting
- Manners
- Meats
- Menus
- Mess
- Microwave
- Mom's cooking

- Most expensive
- Most romantic dinner
- Munchies
- Not closing mouth enough
- Oceans
- Parties around food
- Picnic
- Private parties
- Recipes
- References
- Refrigerator contents
- Refrigerator stories
- Regional foods
- Regrettable meals
- Resorts
- Restaurants
- Rubbish
- Rudest guests
- Rudest meals
- Salt
- Sauces
- School foods
- Seasonings
- Serving dishes

- Shopping stories
- Sickest reaction
- Silverware
- Slurping
- Sodas
- Sparkling
- Spice
- Spills, no thrills
- Starving
- Surprise dinner
- Surprising moment
- Surprising visitors
- Syrup
- Tailgating parties
- Tapas
- Teas
- Thermos
- Traditions around food
- TV food
- Vegetable
- Vegetarian
- Watching another eating
- Water
- White House

- Wines
- Wine: fabulous
- Wine: horrible
- Wine: funny moments
- Wine: funny names
- Wish you were at home
- Yoga
- Yogurt

40: FUNNIEST

Life is not always about being serious, and laughter is an important part of the experience. Below are some prompts to write about your funniest experiences.

- The funniest baby story ...
- The funniest billboard ...
- The funniest book I have read ...
- The funniest comedian I have heard ...
- The funniest construction story is ...
- The funniest couple I have met ...
- The funniest embarrassing moment ...
- The funniest evening playing games ...
- The funniest friend I have had ...
- The funniest jokes I played on others ...
- The funniest jokes played on me ...
- The funniest looking creature I have seen ...
- The funniest moment in my bedroom I experienced ...
- The funniest moment in the bedroom I heard ...
- The funniest moments have been ...
- The funniest movie I saw ...
- The funniest neighborhood story is ...
- The funniest not funny story ...
- The funniest photographic story I heard ...

- The funniest shopping experience ...
- The funniest situation I have been in ...
- The funniest story about animals ...
- The funniest story about cars ...
- The funniest story about clothing ...
- The funniest story about food ...
- The funniest story about my family ...
- The funniest story about traveling ...
- The funniest story remembered in church ...
- The funniest story remembered in school/college ...
- The funniest television program ...
- The funniest thing at a wedding ...
- The funniest thing at home ...
- The funniest thing at my divorce ...
- The funniest thing at my wedding ...
- The funniest thing during a party ...
- The funniest T-shirt ...

41: GIFTS

Gifts are given for all sorts of reasons. What are some of the items you have given as gifts? What are some items you have received as gifts?

Describe the gifts and their significance to you. Do you enjoy giving and receiving gifts? Explain why or why not. These gifts may be in many forms: recipes, patterns, directions, information, jewelry, pictures, books, even advice, counseling and wisdom, etc.

What are some of the oddest gifts you have given or received?

Are there traditions in your family of receiving a certain gift for a particular occasion? Explain. (See Topic 91: TRADITIONS).

42: HEALTH

ADDICTIONS

What is your experience with addiction, either personally or with others, especially those you have been close to? Have you needed to seek help to deal with your own behavior? Have you or a family member been hospitalized, attended AA (Alcoholics Anonymous) or NA (Narcotics Anonymous), or gone to a rehabilitation facility for treatment?

Have there been any accidents, deaths, or close calls due to intoxication or overdoses? If so, how have you dealt with these experiences? (See TOPIC 2: ADDICTIONS & SUBSTANCE ABUSE).

ALLERGIES

Do you have or have you had in the past any allergies?

If yes, what are your allergies? How serious have these allergies been? Have you ever had an allergic reaction? How has it affected your life? Have you ever discovered you no longer have an allergy that previously existed?

Do other members of your family have allergies? Tell about the stories that allergies have created for you and others?

Tell the details of the stories surrounding your medical needs and treatment. Include lists of medications both prescription and over the counter. Do you take any homeopathic medications? (See TOOL SHEET L: HEALTH RECORDS).

MENTAL HEALTH

This is a topic that many do not feel comfortable discussing let alone writing about. Life is difficult. Some of us have had a less complicated life while others have had a constant challenge both mentally and physically.

I encourage you to write about your life and your family and the subject of mental health and illness. You may choose to destroy the material in the end, but it may help you wrap your head around what you experienced. This book is about you and for those you choose to share it with.

What is your family history regarding mental health issues? Have you or a family member ever been hospitalized? What forms of treatment have you and/or your family members received? Have you and/or your family ever taken medication for a mental illness or condition?

Have any conditions, in your opinion, gone undiagnosed?

Have there been any suicides or attempted suicides of family members?

PHYSICAL HEALTH

Describe your physical health history, making note of any serious illnesses, injuries, hospitalizations, conditions, or other facts that are noteworthy.

Note: When we share our personal stories with others, we often find that many others have experienced the same type of event. It may help you to discover that many others share the same experience you have had. Have you ever discovered other people with similar health conditions through disclosing something about yourself?

Have you contracted any serious or chronic diseases in your life? What have you learned about these diseases?

If you have had a serious disease or condition, describe the circumstances in detail, including when you first became aware of it, how soon you sought medical help, and the actual diagnosis, treatment, and duration.

Has there been any history of infertility or childbirth complications?

Describe any serious diseases or conditions that run in your family. Have any individuals in your family been diagnosed with autism or other developmental challenges?

Do you practice preventative medicine, i.e., do you have regular physicals and check-ups? Do you consider yourself a relatively healthy person? Why or why not?

Have you had any elective surgery? Explain how it went. Were there any complications? What was the recovery like, and what suggestions (if any) do you have for others? Do you consider the cycle of the moon before having elective surgery?

ADVICE REGARDING HEALTH

What advice regarding health would you like to offer future generations of your family?

43: HOPES & WISHES

Hopes are what people anticipate might happen. They could be what might come your way or what you have to work hard to obtain. They may be anything from whimsical to concrete. Hope is something anticipated as a possibility.

Wishes, on the other hand, are hopes that are more unlikely to happen. They are often things you cannot always control.

What are your hopes, dreams, and goals for yourself? For others?

How realistic/practical are each of these? What actual steps can be taken and/or completed? Planned?

What time table/schedule do you plan for their fulfillment? What goals have you achieved? Which have been planned? Did they go as scheduled?

What is on your bucket list?

The greatest thing about hopes and wishes are they are free. There is a hidden strength in having them. How do hopes and wishes contribute to your own resilience?

44: HUMOR

- What sort of humor do you appreciate?

- How does humor intertwine in your life?

- Who are your favorite comedians?

- How has having a sense of humor helped you at times in your life?

- Do you appreciate cartoons? If so, which ones? Include your favorite if you have one.

- Do you tell jokes or funny stories? (See TOPIC 54: JOKES).

- Do you have a favorite humorist in literature and art?

- Is there song or music that you remember as being amusing or funny?

- Have you ever experienced a situation where there was laughter that just wouldn't stop?

45: I WILL NEVER FORGET

In life there are those incredible moments you will never forget. They may have been the times when you felt extremely happy or sad, moments that were surprising, or even expected after a long waiting period. Sometimes, we remember something that was seemingly insignificant in the overall scheme of life, but must have been poignant at that particular moment.

List those times in your life that stand out significantly in your memory. When you start writing, you may be reminded of other topics that you have worked on and will think these ideas overlap. When this happens, just go with this notion and write. You may gain a new perspective because of the different approach. Do not resist or overanalyze the situation.

46: IDOLS & SUPERHEROES OF YOUR LIFE

Who have been your idols and superheroes throughout your life? Mention both the idols you have personally known or know through social media, books, storytelling, etc.

47: INHERITANCE

POSSESSIONS

What possessions, money, or other tangible items have you inherited and from whom? Explain their origin and meaning to you and your family.

- Characteristics, physical and behavioral
- Finances
- Intangibles
- Possessions
- Property

GENETICS

What have you inherited and from whom? (See TOPIC 26: DNA)

- Physical traits
- Behavioral tendencies

48: INNER CHILD

The "inner child" is a psychological concept. It is a metaphoric term that refers to the part of people's personalities that is closest to who they were when they were born, which generally includes such qualities as impulsiveness, spontaneity, and creativity. As children grow, they are often barraged by outside expectations. They are told by parents, teachers, and societal institutions how they should think, talk, look, behave, dress and act, as well as what they should value. Often these messages create internal conflicts because people are all unique individuals. Many children grow to adulthood without having fully discovered, let alone having resolved, these internal conflicts.

Proponents of the "inner child" concept suggest that these unaddressed issues and unprocessed emotions do not go away, but rather they are suppressed and reside inside of us as adults, influencing how we see ourselves and the world. They are then handed down to the next generation unless one acknowledges and makes a concerted effort to change.

How do you reclaim and heal your inner child? Regarding materialism, some therapists suggest that people should stop buying superfluous stuff, watching a lot of television, and having so much of their life centered on the material world (which is supposed to make one happy but often leads to only temporary happiness). Instead, they recommend starting connecting or reconnecting with what can give you accurate feedback of who you are. Spend more time in nature, with animals, or by yourself, just being. Remember how to play again. Today many children think playing is using electronics and are attached to devices. True playing is being able to entertain yourself with nature and enjoying others.

The "inner child" requires that you be authentic. You need to accept and love yourself fully. Know who the real you is. Remember the innocence, awe, and wonder of the world. Be able to laugh and run like the free spirit of a child. It is finding the happiness and joyfulness as a young child does by just watching a butterfly fly into the air and disappear. It is finding what makes the little child inside of you joyful again.

Do you have an "inner child" conflict within you? If so, write about how you discovered it and how you have dealt with it.

It often takes hard work and believing in oneself to rediscover a part of this inner child. One exercise that may help is to imagine that you were born the same person as you are today, having the same basic identity, but living in five different countries, and then you all met and communicated. What would be the common denominator that is not cultural? This is the true you. (See TOPIC 4: AFFIRMATIONS).

49: INTERNET

The Internet and the many electronic devices available have become a regular part of most societies. Yet, some of us grew up before the advent of home computers, the Internet, email, and all the benefits, as well as the negative ramifications that have developed.

What was your first experience using a computer? How were computers introduced into your home and work life? Describe the changes that have taken place during your life, while you were going through school, starting to work, or managing a home.

The everyday processes which we access via the Internet are making our lives more convenient than ever; however, the issue of privacy and protecting our identities is also at the forefront of our concerns.

Do you think there may be health issues with these electronic devices so near our bodies?

What are your views and opinions about protecting your own safety, identity, and also your children?

What is your philosophy about the more destructive uses for the Internet that are being employed by groups and individuals who are determined to cause harm to others?

Do you believe it is important to have time away from electronics? Explain.

What do you predict will be changed in 100 years?

50: INTUITION

Having intuition is to understand or know something without true evidence. It is a "just knowing," a feeling that comes to you and you believe in.

- Has intuition been a part of your life?

- If so, how much? When has your intuition been exceptionally strong?

- Did you follow it, or not?

- What were the consequences?

- How often do you follow your intuition? Share your experiences in detail.

- Has your intuition been challenged by other people? Explain.

51: INVENTIONS

Inventions are made due to humanity's desire to better our lives. Over the years inventions have benefited and harmed people, but it is this innate desire to invent that has made the adventure all worth it.

Did you ever come up with an invention for a school project or in your adult life? If so, what was your invention? Include photos and documents. Have you or any family members invented something? Were any actually sold? What have you thought about inventing?

For each of the inventions in the following list, give your opinion about them, i.e., whether or not they are good for our society or harmful. Rating: 1 = Terrible to 5 = Great. How have they changed your life? Write down any stories that come to you.

- Air conditioning
- Automobiles
- Birth control
- Cellular phones
- Compact discs
- Computer mouse
- Computers
- Cordless tools
- Digital cameras
- Digital clocks
- Digital music

- DNA testing
- Electric curlers-irons
- Electric hair dryer
- Fabric softener
- Fast food
- Faster air travel
- Fingerprinting
- GPS
- Heart transplants
- High speed Internet
- In-vitro fertilization

- Jet plane
- Laser surgery
- Latex paint
- LED
- Medicines
- Microwave
- MRI
- Remote controls
- Robots
- Satellite
- Smoke detectors
- Sneakers
- Solar heat
- Space travel
- Super glue
- Synthetic fabrics
- Television
- Uni-size
- Unisex
- Video games
- Video recorders

52: JACK-IN-THE-BOX

Share those surprises in your life that you never expected. For example, finding out you have a half-sister at your father's funeral; or that the water pipes broke in your home when you were on vacation, etc.

53: JIGSAW PUZZLE

A jigsaw puzzle is when you know in your gut you are missing information that you need to fully understand a situation, yet you are curious about the details. Finally the missing piece of information comes to light, and you have the feeling of "Oh, now I understand!"

Have you had intuitions that did not make sense for a period of time, perhaps years, and then you found the missing piece of information, making everything very clear? Explain in detail.

54: JOKES

Some people think of themselves as comedians, and others love jokes but do not like to tell them. Others are writers and illustrators of jokes.

Tell the best or worst jokes you know or the only three you know. Rate them 1 = Worst and 5 = Best.

55: KALEIDOSCOPE IMAGE

Similar to a kaleidoscope, we all have life experiences of the multifaceted angles and situations of our life. We each interpret them in our own unique way. Write about or create color pictures of your life and the many changes you have experienced. Please interpret them.

Note each color is known for its characteristics:

- Red   = passion, energy or heat;
- Green   = wisdom or earthiness;
- Yellow   = happiness, joy, hope, sunshine, jealousy;
- Orange   = warning, balance, attention;
- Blue   = infinity, trust, water and sky;
- Purple   = royalty and the ethereal;
- Brown   = earthiness;
- Pink   = romance and love;
- Beige   = quietness and calm;
- Black   = mystery or death and rebirth.
- White   = purity and innocence.

56: LEGAL SITUATIONS

The legal system has many flaws, and at times, decisions and outcomes are not always fair. The courts exist in order to bring some kind of settlement between two opposing forces, usually people or businesses. Here is a place to share your experiences. (See TOPIC 17: CRIME—CIVIL & CRIMINAL and TOOL SHEET N: LEGAL FACTS).

Consider the legal encounters and court cases you have experienced. The courthouse is an amazing place. Just attending court is an educational experience, whether you are involved or as a spectator. Highlight the case, the lawyers' roles, what they did or did not do, the situation, influences, and results. How did you feel about the case? Describe the day before going to court, entering the courthouse, leaving the courthouse, and after receiving the final decision.

If the case was settled without a hearing, did it get as far as the courtroom or not? What was the decision, and how do you feel about not having it heard in court? If you had it to do over, what would you do differently? What did you learn?

Have you ever been on jury duty? Was it federal or state court? How have your experiences influenced your perception of justice, judges, lawyers, and courtroom procedures?

Share your thoughts about your legal situations as well as about

- Adoption

- Being sued

- Boundary lines

- Child custody

- Court cases

- Defendants

- Divorce

- Jury duty

- Lawyer experiences

- Legal battles

- Legal documents

- Legal issues regarding health issues

- Legal issues regarding real estate

- Plaintiffs

- Star witness

- Suing

- Trusts

- Wills

57: LETTERS—TO AND FROM

What are the special letters you have received, mailed, or written and never mailed?

Do you have the originals or copies of these letters?-Have you made copies or scan the letters and include with them the dates when they were written and your age.

Have you bought or read the published letters/correspondence of famous people? What letters/correspondence are your favorite?

Have you written letters to those who have meant a lot to you? Have you written letters for individuals to be shared after your funeral?

58: LIFE PREPARATIONS FOR YOUR FAMILY

What preparations have you made for the possibility of illness and your eventual death, as well as the possibility of living for a time when you may not be able to make decisions? Where are these papers located? (See TOOL SHEET F: DEATH).

Which documents have you prepared, and who was your attorney?

- Health Care Proxy
- Funeral Directives
- Living Will or Advance Directive
- Medical Records
- Music
- Pre-nuptial
- Obituary
- Trusts
- Will

Have you made plans for a funeral or memorial service?

- Burial plot purchased or place of rest
- Cremation or burial

59: LIFESTYLE

What was your lifestyle growing up? What is your lifestyle now? What experiences, events, attitudes, trends, level of education, or careers have played a role in determining your lifestyle? Did you change your lifestyle from how you were raised? If yes, was there something or someone who influenced you strongly enough for you to decide to make a major change? (See TOPIC 29: ENVIRONMENT & REAL ESTATE).

Write down the year and your age at the time of the experience.

Describe your lifestyle in relation to these topics:

- Career or lack thereof
- Children
- Choice in type of home you live in. Do/did you rent or own?
- Community involvement
- Financial matters
- Friends
- Involvement in sports

- Leisure time
- Relationships
- Religion
- Second home or time share
- Social life
- Transportation
- Volunteering
- Where do/have you lived

60: LITERATURE

What are your favorite poems, books, articles? Include them here and explain why you find them so fascinating or as good friends of the soul.

Which of the following books have you read? How old were you when you read them?

- *The Adventures of Huckleberry Finn* by Mark Twain
- *The Divine Comedy* by Dante Alighieri
- *The Great Gatsby* by F. Scott Fitzgerald
- *War and Peace* by Leo Tolstoy
- *Crime and Punishment* by Fyodor Dostoevsky
- *Alice's Adventures in Wonderland* by Lewis Carroll
- *Pride and Prejudice* by Jane Austen
- *The Catcher in the Rye* by J. D. Salinger
- *Wuthering Heights* by Emily Bronte
- *The Iliad* by Homer
- *Catch-22* by Joseph Heller
- *Invisible Man* by Ralph Ellison
- *As I Lay Dying* by William Faulkner
- *Portrait of the Artist as a Young Man* by James Joyce
- *The Scarlet Letter* by Nathaniel Hawthorne

And so many others ... List the books that have been most influential in your life.

If you could take a year of your life and be in any book as one of the characters, who would you be in what book?

61: LOVE, HATRED, & INDIFFERENCE

In life we usually experience different kinds of love. What was your first memory of having feelings of love or being loved? For many, it began with family, pets, and friends. For others, it was a person outside of the family. Tell about the most significant loves in your life.

There is platonic love and romantic love. Describe the difference between loving and being in love. When have you fallen in love? Who was it? How old were you? What were your experiences with each other? What made this person so special? Have you been betrayed? If so explain.

Do you believe in love at first sight? Do you believe in the idea of a "soul mate"? Do you believe that some lovers had known each other in a previous life? Have you ever felt this way? If so, describe in detail.

Often after being in love there is a falling out for various reasons. Often anger, frustration, hatred and disappointment are brought out. If you have experienced this, please explain. (See TOPIC 55: KALEIDOSCOPE IMAGE and TOOL SHEET P: MARRIAGE, ENGAGEMENT, SIGNIFICANT OTHERS, SEPARATION, & DIVORCE).

To you what is fascination? Affection? Admiration? Romance? Sex? Sensuality? Pillow talk?

The opposite of love is indifference. Have you reached this feeling with someone you once loved?

62: MIRRORING

Mirroring is something we do both consciously and unconsciously. It is about better understanding who we are. In many relationships you learn more about yourself as you interact with another. They naturally challenge you as a person. You get angry when they push your buttons, even if they did not intentionally do so. It is through this reflecting, on how you feel and respond to a situation, that you learn about yourself. Once you recognize your feelings and responses, you can either stay the same or you can make the conscious choice to react differently. Sometimes we learn from a childhood experience that we had and now feel we can respond differently to it.

This sort of change can be started by looking in the mirror and seeing yourself more deeply. What is it that makes you tick? How do you choose to present yourself through your behavior, clothes, and appearance?

An example of this is if someone upsets you and you respond with annoyance or anger. You may ask yourself, "What is it about that person that is upsetting me?" It's not uncommon to discover that the things we dislike about others are things we dislike about ourselves and our own behaviors. Our responses are as much about ourselves as the other person.

Mirroring can also be about when you encounter a person who makes you happy after a challenging time in your life. These experiences can bring out the YOU that existed before you buried your joyfulness and they can remind you of the happier moments of life. (See TOOL SHEET D: CHARACTERISTICS OF STRENGTH AND CHALLENGES).

How do others react to your presence?

When you enter a room or building, do others notice you? How does it change the feeling of the room?

How does the presence of others affect you?

- Have you ever caught yourself unconsciously emulating or acting like the people you spend time with?

- What habits or behaviors of others have you taken up on purpose?

- Is your behavior being influenced by another person currently?

What have others told you about yourself?

- Surprising compliments

- Surprising put-downs or criticisms

- Recurring comments or observations from multiple sources

What are your negative impressions of yourself?

- Personality flaws

- Weaknesses

- Annoying habits

What are your positive ideas or images about yourself?

- Strengths

- Personality quirks

- Positive habits

63: MOVIE OF YOUR LIFE

"YOUR LIFE" is now playing at the local theaters.

If you were going to produce a movie about your life, describe the specific genre of the film. Would it be a drama? Romantic comedy? Action film? Science fiction?

What would the movie be called? Write a new review of the movie after the first week of airing.

Name some actors/actresses who would best portray you as a young child, a teenager, young adult, and an older adult? What specifically would be important for them to know in order to personify your character?

Please list the main characters in "YOUR LIFE" and who would play those roles. Explain in detail why you made these choices.

64: MUSIC & DANCE

How has music been a part of your life? Did you learn to play an instrument(s)? If so, when did you start to play an instrument? Did you have lessons or were you self-taught? Tell about your learning experiences (See TOOL SHEET Q: MUSIC & DANCE).

Were you ever part of a choir or singing group? Tell about that experience of singing with others or on your own. Did you ever sing publicly?

Were music lessons offered at school when you were a child? Describe the room where the lessons were taught. Who was your teacher? Did you like this activity at school? Did your parents insist that you take part, or did you want to take these lessons?

When you were growing up was music played in your home? If yes what genres were played? Did someone in your family enjoy playing an instrument, and did this influence you? What did your parents think about the music you liked?

Who were the famous musicians and bands of your time when you were growing up? Did your siblings and close friends like the same music as you? If not, what was their preference?

What genres of music do you enjoy now? How has the way you listen to music now changed from when you were a child? Describe your listening devices over the years. What music do you not like? Explain.

What other memories do you have of music being in your life?

65: NAMES—WHAT IS IN A NAME?

How do you choose a baby's name? By the sound, the initials, family tradition, place, after a special person, or a name you have always loved? Does your family have traditions in choosing names? Please explain in detail. Do the corresponding initials affect your decision-making process when choosing a name?

What are the consequences of having a certain name? Do you think being given a certain name can influence the kind of person you become, how others treat you, or other issues? Did you have a nickname, and if yes, how did it come about? How did you feel about your nickname?

If you could choose your own name, what would your full name be? Have you changed your name? If so, what was your former name? Why did you change your name?

When naming a child do you take into consideration what the name will sound like when you are disciplining them or when there will be a romantic moment? Have you given a nickname to another person? If yes, explain in detail. Speaking about nicknames, have you ever wondered why one chooses one name and then uses another? Have you ever wondered how a name ending in anything but a "Y" sound often ends up with a "Y" ending name?

How do you decide what name to call a child or pet? If you had 12 children, 6 girls and 6 boys, what names would you give them? How did you choose these names? What names do you love/dislike and why?

66: NATURAL ENVIRONMENT

What are your feelings about the natural environment? What is your connection with nature? How important is nature to you and why? Write about these adventures during your childhood through adulthood. If you had limited access to nature, why is this and how do you feel about this lack of exposure? Have you changed the situation? If so, how?

Do you enjoy gardening? Have you grown flowers and/or vegetables? Do you enjoy being near mountains, plains, rainforests, the ocean, lakes, and ponds? Have you lived where there are distinct different seasons of the year? What changes in nature do you enjoy with each season? Write about your most memorable seasons, years, months, and holidays with the environment playing a strong role. What sports do or have you participated in that depended on nature?

Explain any natural environmental knowledge or beliefs you have. What are your beliefs regarding nature?

Tell about any natural disasters you have experienced directly or that affected your life through the media or through family and friends.

Do you have favorite writings, songs, or experiences regarding nature? Have you written about nature? If so, please include (See TOOL SHEET R: NATURE).

67: ORGANIZATIONS & MEMBERSHIPS

What organizations or memberships has your family been active in? Were they involved with the needs of people, animals, the arts, or hobbies such as motorcycle groups? What roles have you played within these organizations? Do you consider it important to contribute time and to be a member of an organization? What suggestions do you have regarding being a part of an organization? Did any of these organizations have an influence on you? Explain (See TOOL SHEET A: ACTIVITIES, COLLECTIBLES, HOBBIES, INTERESTS, & SPORTS).

68: ORGANIZING

People have different priorities regarding organizing. What is your philosophy regarding organizing? If you are in a room that is organized or not organized, does this affect your ability to feel comfortable? How was your home when you were growing up/now? How does organization relate to your daily life?

Have you organized a group? Do you feel that organizing a group comes to you naturally? What have you learned through your experiences of organizing? What suggestions can you offer to others regarding being an organizer?

How well organized is your living and working environment? What are some of your secrets solutions for organizing?

69: PEOPLE

CHARACTERS I HAVE KNOWN

Who are the unusual and unique individuals that you remember for being themselves—whether they are funny, kind, sincere, authentic, bizarre, or brilliant—the eccentric ones? They may be members of your family, community, or world figures; or they may be fictitious figures from books, comics, movies, or stories that had an important impact on your life. These individuals include historical figures, great thinkers, athletes, religious leaders, and heroes. They may or may not have influenced you, but they did not pass without notice (See TOOL SHEETS D: CHARACTERISTICS, H: EMPLOYMENT-SELF EMPOYMENT-JOBS, and S: PEOPLE).

FRIENDS

List your special friends; explain when and how you met them. How old were you and what year was it? What was the attraction or common denominator on which your friendship was built? Do you know where they are today? How close are they to you now? Describe your relationship with them today. Who are your closest friends today?

What friends do you have that you have not seen for years, yet you know if you were to see them it would be as if you had seen them yesterday?

INFLUENTIAL PEOPLE/MENTORS

Who have been some of the most influential people in your life? Have you ever been mentored by someone? (See TOOL SHEET D: CHARACTERISTICS).

Did/do they know of their influence on your life? Have you given them verbal acknowledgement? What kind of mentor would you have wanted that you did not get? Do you know if you have been another's mentor? If yes, how did you come to understand this acknowledgement?

Who are the important people in your life who have earned your respect?

NEIGHBORS

We all have had experiences with neighbors. Tell about your experiences with neighbors, past and present. (See your LIFE CALENDAR and TOOL SHEET D: CHARACTERISTICS).

OTHER PEOPLE IN YOUR LIFE

As you read the list on TOOL SHEET D: CHARACTERISTICS, see your LIFE CALENDAR and write down the names that come to mind, including yourself, or whoever fits beside that word. Note: Not all the words will produce a name and that is fine. It is not a test but an exercise to bring back the people in your life. After you have completed the list, reread it with the understanding that this is who the person is and they will most likely not change.

PROFESSIONALS, DOCTORS, LAWYERS

Were your parents professionals in their fields of work?

Who are some of the professional people from whom you have sought advice or help? Who are/were your primary care physicians or other medical professionals? Do you have an attorney, accountant, or other professionals that you work with on a regular basis? How did you choose the people you work with? (See your LIFE CALENDAR and TOOL SHEET D: CHARACTERISTICS).

WHO IS

Let us jog your memory about various people who have caught your attention and made an impression over time for one reason or another. Using TOOL SHEET D: CHARACTERISTICS, name some people who first come to mind. Include acquaintances, family, friends, literary characters, people in the media, and others.

70: PHILOSOPHY OF AGING

One guarantee in life is that once we are born we will have an ending.

What is your family's health history and typical longevity? (See TOPIC 42: HEALTH and TOOL SHEET L: HEALTH RECORDS). Have you had any life challenges so far? What precautionary measures are you taking to prevent illness? What is your daily routine regarding diet and exercising?

Have you helped any elderly people in your life through work or on a personal level? What words of wisdom have they shared with you?

Have you prepared for the time when you grow older? What happens if something out of your control happens? Do you have family who can help physically, financially, and emotionally? There is a new term for adult people in this situation. They are called "adult orphans." Have you made any preparations regarding your future and possible health surprises or accidents?

There are many ways one can alter one's home in order to stay longer, to have an independent lifestyle, such as stairway lifts. There are several different kinds of facilities to take care of the elderly, if you can afford to pay for one. Also there are state facilities in the USA. Have you made any preparations for yourself or any other family members?

Do you have a living will? A will? A trust? Have you gone over these things with your existing family or with anyone?

Share your thoughts about elderly care and the philosophy of aging in your country.

71: PHOTOGRAPHS

PERSONAL PHOTOGRAPHS

Photographs are a great place to start to evoke a feeling and experiences to write about. Photographs portray a history of your family and your life. You may have older prints or slides of your family or others, or of travel destinations and places your family has lived. Have you established a method of categorizing these photos? If the photos cannot be identified, are there family members who might know who is in the photo or when and where it was taken? Are your old photos being well preserved?

With digital photographs, it is important to take the time to make edits and include pertinent information regarding each individual photo. Do you have back-up files for these photos—on your property as well as offsite? You might want to consider making photograph albums for your children, including photos of your wedding, their grandparents, them as babies, and other family members that they might not remember as they grow older. You could also include photos of their artwork, houses you lived in, places visited, schools attended, report cards, vehicles, awards, pets, cars, best friends, and some personal possessions or toys.

One way to organize your photos is to have them organized into groups by using sequential numbers as part of the new name you give them. For example, the first part of the name is divided as follows: place the number 2 in front of all photography that are beautiful by location; 3 for family members; 4 for real estate and personal inventory; 5 for friends; 6 for business. The following code would be the place or family in the photo. For example: 5_Jenny_2017-03-05 WY_100. The first number tells it is a friend; the second information "Jenny" tells me which friend; the next is the year, month, and day it was taken; the "WY" tells me we were in Wyoming. This format keeps your photos in chronological order. Next you place them into a folder using the same method.

Note: When you copy a .jpg the computer usually decreases the quality. It is highly suggested that you put original photos on a hard drive then keep the copies in the "cloud" or use another method. Keep the originals for photo albums and to display or give as gifts. Always have two backups kept in separate locations.

Now, with the inclusion of cameras in cell phones and all the new apps, photos can be taken anytime and anywhere. Do be sure to take videos too. Try to capture your experiences. These clips will help you write your memoirs in great detail.

PUBLIC PHOTOGRAPHS

Photographs are no longer rare treasures but available instantly with the new phone devices. How has this affected our life? Has it been an intrusion to our privacy? How has capturing brutal police behavior and other scenarios helped better inform the public? YouTube has been an incredible way to communicate throughout the world. Its content ranges from simple videos on how use your camera to amazing sporting event. There are also beautiful moments captured regarding the animal kingdom and their unique behaviors. How do you feel about this? What boundaries or limits should be place on photography?

72: PLAY

Playing is a time to enjoy yourself. Play may look like participating in a sport or game, or it may be just talking and laughing with your family around a BBQ grill. It might be crawling on the floor with your one year old. Play does create a time when you can relax and not be worried.

- In what ways do you create playtime?

- Who do you love to play with the most?

- What was your experience regarding play while you were growing up?

- What percentage of your waking time do you currently play today?

- Explain what your beliefs and habits are regarding playing.

73: POLITICS

While governments vary from democracies to dictatorships, most provide laws, a system for common defense, and economic policies. Throughout history, many people's lives have been irrevocably changed because of their country's government.

What is the political structure of the country in which you grew up and/or now live? What was the past political history of this country? Who were its leaders? Do you still live in the country in which you were born? If not, did you/your family leave because of the government or its policies?

Are you politically active? Do you identify with a particular political party? Have you ever participated in a political campaign? If so, in what capacity and for whom?

If you live in the United States, what image comes to mind when you hear the word Republican? Democrat? Independent?

When you were growing up, were politics discussed in your home? Did everyone in your family have similar political views and support the same candidates? If not, how did differing political views impact family dynamics?

Do you have a favorite political cartoon or joke? Describe it or print a copy.

Which politician(s) do you admire the most? Why?

Which politician(s) do you admire least? Why?

While most of us are impacted by a wide variety of laws and policies made by our government, is there one particular law or policy that has had a major impact on your life, for better or for worse? If so, which one and why?

World leaders and intellectuals have discussed and argued about politics for thousands of years. Read the quotations below. Do you agree or disagree with them? Use these quotations as inspiration to write about your own experiences with government or its policies, or write your own quotable quote about government.

- "A state is better governed which has few laws, and those laws strictly observed."—René Descartes

- "The most terrifying words in the English language are: I'm from the government and I'm here to help."—Ronald Reagan

- "A nation of sheep will beget a government of wolves."—Edward R. Murrow

- "The problem with socialism is that you eventually run out of other peoples' money."—Margaret Thatcher

- "As government expands, liberty contracts."—Ronald Reagan

- "The Constitution is not an instrument for the government to restrain the people, it is an instrument for the people to restrain the government - lest it come to dominate our lives and interests."—Patrick Henry

- "Let us never forget that government is ourselves and not an alien power over us. The ultimate rulers of our democracy are not a President and senators and congressmen and government officials, but the voters of this country."—Franklin D. Roosevelt

- "Anyone who knows history, particularly the history of Europe, will, I think, recognize that the domination of education or of government by any one particular religious faith is never a happy arrangement for the people."—Eleanor Roosevelt

How do current political issues (abortion, same-sex marriage, education, environmental regulations, wages, economics, taxes, gun laws, immigration, and health) affect your personal life?

74: PREFER THIS OR THAT

Each line has two options. Please put a check beside your preferences. See how your family members are like or different from you. Do any of the comments bring life stories to mind? Please write about them.

	Republican		Democrat
	Legalizing marijuana		Against legalizing marijuana
	Believe in God		Atheist or Agnostic
	Attending religious services		No formal religious services
	Daily prayers		No prayers
	Save money		Do not save money
	Wear wedding ring		Do not wear wedding ring
	Burial in a casket		Cremation
	Give money to a street musician		Choose not to give money to a street musician
	Give money to a beggar		Choose not to give money to a beggar
	Listening to a friend's troubles		Prefer not to listen to friend's troubles
	Going for the most		Going for the least
	Have library card		Do not use library
	Purchase a book		Take book out from library
	Write ten letters per year		Write less than ten letters per year

	Send holiday cards		Do not send holiday cards
	Read 15+ books per year		Read less than 15 books per year
	Read novels		Read non-fiction
	Prefer travel books		Prefer books about sports
	Prefer reading about mythology		Prefer reading war stories
	Prefer reading about animals		Prefer reading fairy tales
	Prefer a book of jokes		Prefer reading a biography
	Prefer National Geographic		Prefer a woman's magazine
	Prefer National Geographic		Prefer Sports Illustrated
	Prefer reading poetry		Prefer reading stories
	Willing to take part in a survey		Do not participate in surveys
	Reading		Attending a party
	Attending a party		Staying at home
	Being alone		Being with people
	Unlisted phone number		Listed phone number
	Being inside		Being outside
	Country living		Urban living
	Warm climate		Cold climate
	Live east of the Mississippi		Live west of the Mississippi
	Own home		Rent home

	Single family home		Condo/apartment
	Lakeside home		Ocean front home
	Contemporary home		Traditional home
	Pastel colors in décor		Primary colors in décor
	Window shades		Window curtains
	Hardwood floors		Carpeted floors
	Fireplace/Wood stove		No wood burning device
	Forced hot air		Forced steam/baseboard
	Interior temperature kept at 68°		Interior temperature kept at 72°
	Overhead lights in a room		Prefer candle light
	Firm mattress		Soft mattress
	Poly-filled pillows		Down/feather pillows
	Down comforter		Blankets
	Wear night-clothes to bed		Sleep in the nude
	Wear swim suit		Prefer nude swimming
	Wearing clothes		Not wearing clothing
	Use fabric softener		Do not use fabric softener
	Bath		Shower
	Early morning riser/early to bed		Sleep in morning/stay up late
	Wash hair daily		Wash hair 2-3 times per week

	Weigh self weekly		Weigh self monthly
	Brush teeth 1-2 times per day		Brush teeth 3-4 times per day
	Organized		Disorganized
	More comfortable in T-shirts		Prefer more formal shirt/top
	Costume jewelry		Gold/silver/gem stones
	Athletic shoes		Dress shoes
	Shoes		Barefoot
	One ring per hand		More than one ring per hand
	Recycle regularly		Dispose recyclable material
	Use riding lawn mower		Use push mower
	Transportation by train		Transportation by air
	Driving oneself		Being driven
	Ordering an automobile		Getting an automobile off the lot
	Memorized driver's license number		Have not memorized driver's license number
	American automobile		Foreign automobile
	Car		Truck
	Sports car		Sport utility/wagon
	Red car		Tan car
	Two one-week vacations		One two-week vacation

	Camping in a tent		Camping in an RV
	Camping in the mountains		Camping at the beach
	Tennis		Golf
	Lake/Ocean swimming		Pool swimming
	Running outside		Running inside on a track
	Soccer		Football
	Doodling while on the phone		Not doodling while on the phone
	Purchase lottery tickets		Never purchase lottery tickets
	Watch television game show		Watch television soap opera
	Watch football on television		Watch old movie on television
	Watch television show		Watch a video
	Watch television		Listen to radio
	Shop at a mall		Shop at specialty stores
	Shop/order through catalogues		Shop by visiting stores in person
	Shop when visiting a city		Search out historic places when visiting a city
	Three cups of coffee per day or less		More than three cups of coffee per day
	Sugar		Artificial sweetener
	Salt on food		No salt on food
	Tea		Coffee

	Herbal tea		Black tea
	Pepsi		Coke
	Juice		Water
	Drinking from a glass		Drinking from a plastic cup
	Prefer to eat poultry		Prefer fish
	White chicken meat		Dark chicken meat
	Frozen yogurt		Ice cream
	Mashed potatoes		Rice
	Brown rice		White rice
	Oil and vinegar dressing		Blue cheese dressing
	Restaurant meals		Home-cooked meals
	Sandwich cut into rectangles		Sandwich cut into triangles
	Having a house cleaner		Having a cook
	Cooking		Cleaning
	Carry photos in wallet		No photos in wallet
	Purchase a Christmas tree		Cut your own Christmas tree
	Own pets		Do not own pets
	Big dogs		Little dogs
	Glad this is the last question?		Wish there were more questions?

75: PREJUDICE & RACISM

As people we usually have strong opinions about life, other people, and life philosophies. One of the results of this is prejudice and racism.

Have you grown up experiencing prejudice of any kind? Do you have any firsthand knowledge or have you experienced any turbulent times when issues of race and prejudice were being challenged? Have you felt prejudice due to your religion, sexual orientation, race, sex, or age? Explain. Where did the feeling originate? Was it through family beliefs or an experience? Do you want to choose to hold onto this belief or to change?

What do you think needs to change to eradicate racism and prejudice? How do you see yourself? Do you sense that you have racist or prejudicial tendencies? Can anyone be totally free from prejudice?

What is your general philosophy about the current racial tensions, immigration policies, discrimination, and political climate that are present in your society? Remember to record the year that you are writing about and the current issues that are at the forefront of the times.

76: QUIZ OF THE FUTURE

How do you imagine the future? What would you like to have different or stay the same? What do you imagine for future generations?

In the YEAR OF ____ (add 50 years from this date), I predict

- Food will
- Work will
- Pets will
- Homes will
- Space will
- Manners will
- Schools will
- Families will
- Fashions will
- Entertainment will
- Transportation will
- Children's playing will
- The environment will
- The electronic world will provide

77: QUOTES

What are some of your favorite quotes? When did you discover them? These are words either written or heard that have great meaning for you and your life. Be sure to give credit to the person and/or book.

Quote yourself as well. Remember things you have said to others or written.

78: REALITY TV

Television networks have created a great deal of entertainment called "reality TV" shows. These shows feature regular people or celebrities and place them in a challenging setting, or they portray people's everyday lives. The common theme is that the shows are largely unscripted.

Why do these shows exist?

Are they really "reality"? Are they exaggerated individuals creating a show for the general public to live vicariously through the characters?

How do you feel about "reality" TV?

79: RELATIONSHIPS

Remember that you can start to work from any place in the book at any time. You may encounter similar questions for which you might recall a slightly different perspective.

During our life we encounter many reltionships with people.

Define the following relationships

- Friendship
- Acquaintance
- Best friends
- Professional relationship
- Long-distance relationship
- Significant other
- Friends with benefits
- Marriage
- Estranged
- Ex
- Enemy

Describe personal relationships

- Friends
- Acquaintances
- Best friends
- Professional people

- Long-distance relationship

- Significant other

- Friends with benefits

- Marriage

- Estranged

- Ex

- Enemy

80: SCARY TIMES

What were some moments in your life that were scary? Were they in the form of a nightmare or real-life experiences? Were they actual, dangerous situations or threats of danger coming? Were they created by mankind or nature itself or a combo (for example, you skied and caused an avalanche)?

List these times and then try to give detailed descriptions, again using the five senses (See TOPIC 35: FEARS & SHAMES and the LIFE CALENDAR).

81: SCIENCE FICTION

Science fiction and other speculative genres help people expand their imagination and live fantasies via books or cinema that they couldn't possibly live in their current life.

- Do you like science fiction? What forms of movies, books, artwork, or video games do you enjoy?

- What books have you read?

- What movies have you seen?

- What feelings do they provoke?

- What was it about each of these book/movies that drew you to watch them?

- Did any of them influence you in any way?

- What fascinates you about science fiction?

- What science fiction movies and/or books do you dislike? Explain.

- If you were to write a science fiction story, write a brief synopsis here.

- If you could be a superhero, who would you be and why?

82: SELF-PORTRAIT

You are about to have a portrait of yourself created. What message would you like to be told or essence of you portrayed? What do you want people to think of you from seeing your portrait?

When having a portrait done, you can create the atmosphere in which you will be portrayed. Thus what are the following things you would include or like to have illustrated?

- What is your choice for the medium used (oils, watercolors, clay sculpture...)?

- At what age are you?

- What is your stance/position?

- Is it full-figured or partial? Frontal or three-quarters facing?

- What expression is on your face?

- What is your attire?

- What props do you have?

- What is the location? Indoors or outdoors?

- What size?

- What style or period of art does this reflect?

- Is it formal or casual?

- Are there other people or pets in the picture?

- What is the message you are sending to the viewer?

Try sketching a self-portrait. If you have already attempted to make a self-portrait, include it here. Have you had someone do your portrait? You could also include a collage of different photos or pictures.

83: SEX

When did you become aware of the difference between the sexes, sensuality, and sexuality? How did you learn about sex and sensuality? What was your understanding then and now of sex and sensuality?

Who was the first person to touch you in a sexual and/or sensual way? What was that experience like for you? At what age did you become sexually active? What was happening in your peer group at that time? Were your friends experimenting with sex? Were you able to approach your parents or siblings with questions regarding sexuality? How did you become educated? Were you able to speak with friends, family, professionals, either your doctor or Planned Parenthood or another organization?

What were your family's beliefs? Community expectations? Was there sex education in your school? Did your family's religious beliefs influence your thoughts and behavior regarding sex?

Did you experience any traumas related to a sexual and sensual experience? Have you or any members of your family ever been sexually assaulted? How has this affected you and your feelings about sensuality and sexuality? (SEE TOPIC 84: SEXUAL ORIENTATION AND GENDER IDENTIFICATION).

84: SEXUAL ORIENTATION & GENDER IDENTIFICATION

There are many words, acronyms, and terminology being used today to describe different sexual orientations and gender identities. Here are some terms to help you describe yourself and those with whom you have close relationships.

Times change so rapidly; you may describe yourself in today's terms, but these terms might be obsolete thirty or sixty years from now when someone in your family might be reading this.

Do you identify as:

- Bisexual: Attracted to people of both sexes, physically, emotionally, and sexually

- Gay: Attracted to people of your own sex

- Lesbian: If you are female, and are only attracted to other females

- Friend to LGBTQ: Supportive of the lesbian, gay, bisexual or transgender, or queer community at large

- Queer: The "Q" in the LGBTQ community, in some way not heteronormative

- Straight: Attracted to people of the opposite sex; heterosexual

- Transgender: You do not identify with the sex you were born, but this does not imply that you identify with any particular sexual orientation.

If you are not straight, have you been able to "come out" to your family about your sexual orientation? If not, what has held you back?

Have you been a victim of harassment or discrimination because of your sexual orientation or gender identity?

Have you had family or close friends that have a different sexual orientation or gender identity than you?

Are you the parent, sibling, or child of someone who is a part of the LGBTQ community? Are you able to be supportive of your family member(s)? (See TOPIC 83: SEX).

85: SKELETONS

Skeletons are facts or incidents in our past that people try to hide or ignore. It may be because of shame, embarrassment, or self-judgment.

How do you see yourself reconciling with your skeletons? Perhaps writing would help. You can then choose to keep the writings or not. We all have skeletons; some are from family, and others we may have created ourselves. And some are incidents that happened to us.

86: SPORTS, EXERCISE, & FITNESS

SPORTS

Have sports, individual and/or organized, been a part of your life and your family? Write about the sports and other activities in which you have been involved and your experiences. (See TOOL SHEET A: ACTIVITIES, HOBBIES, INTERESTS, COLLECTIBLES & SPORTS).

- Sport or activity:

- Age when you started:

- Costs involved with sport:

- Team sport, club, or league?

- Team colors and mascot?

- Was special training or coaching necessary?

- Do you have photographs/videos of yourself playing this sport?

- Do you have any newspaper clippings or other news releases mentioning your name?

- Did you keep a journal of the time you spent involved with this sport?

- Did you play this sport competitively/professionally?

- Did a professional athlete influence you?

EXERCISE & FITNESS

What types of exercise do you enjoy the most?

Do you believe that it is important to exercise and stay fit? How have you integrated exercise and physical fitness into your life? Where do you fit on the spectrum of being extremely fit to being sedentary? What years of your life have you been the most active? If your activity level has changed over the years, explain why.

What has your weight been over the years? Has your weight changed? If your weight has changed, what were the causes? Explain in detail.

Have you tried dieting or specific weight-loss or weight-gain plans? Were they successful?

Do you feel you have enough knowledge regarding fitness and exercise? How important is maintaining a certain level of fitness to you?

87: STORYTELLING

Have you any memories of listening to stories? Who were the people who narrated these stories? When and where did these activities take place?

Depending on when you were born, you most likely listened to stories on the radio or via tape or CD. Today it might be through iTunes or some other electronic application. Do you listen to stories while driving or in your home? Did you attend a "story hour" at your local library or school? Did your family read to you?

Do you remember any stories you were told that made a strong impression on you in some way? Explain and tell if a certain character was particularly impressive.

Do you have any family stories that were told? Please write them down to share.

88: TATTLETALES

Ask your close friends if they have any stories or memories about your family and your life. Meet with them and discuss these stories. Jot notes or perhaps record the conversation (get permission to record the conversation). You can ask if they would be willing to write one or two memories down. Include your findings.

- From:
- Address:
- Email:
- Telephone:
- Year you met:
- How old you were when you met:
- Details of their story:

89: TECHNOLOGY

Like computers and the Internet, technology has transformed many aspects of our lives. The idea that the introduction of new machines, faster transportation, more efficient methods of shopping, and so forth would help us save time and make many tasks easier has in many respects created just the opposite effect. We find ourselves being stimulated by so much incoming information that we are becoming addicted to the technology itself, be it video games, shopping, self-diagnosing, researching, or using social media. We have created more things to do and to get done. We spend less time talking with each other in person, and more time looking at our devices.

How have you integrated existing technology into your present life? Can you think of ways in which technology has had a positive influence on your life? Can you think of ways in which technology has had a negative influence on your life? What innovations do you depend on in your daily life? What are some that you think are harmful?

Reflecting on this concept, do you believe your life is better because of technology? Please explain. What do you think the new technology of the year 2050 will look like? Will we have cars that drive us? Will we become creatures having little eye contact with others, as we can get everything done through our devices?

What do you envision in the future? How do you imagine your children's lives will be different than yours as a result of technology? Do you think that we will discover that there are physical detriments from these devices?

As an alternative, list the pros and cons of new technology in regard to health, relationships, school work, finances, career, raising children, law enforcement, and/or privacy.

90: TESTS

MANDATORY TESTS

There are tests you are required to take to further your education, to be able to drive a vehicle, to become a professional, to receive your degree, or to gain employment in certain fields. What tests have you had? What were your scores? How did they affect you?

SPECIAL INTEREST TESTS

On this page list any tests you have taken, including special interest, psychological, or professional tests.

Explain the tests you have taken and what you learned about yourself. Do you like tests?

- Test:

- Reason for test:

- Date:

- Your age:

- Who conducted the test and where was it taken?

- Score or outcome:

- Aptitudes you have:

91: TRADITIONS

Each culture has its traditions. Each family has its traditions. It is a way to celebrate special occasions as well as how you live your daily life.

List your family traditions regarding ...

- Behavior

- Customs

- Food

- Gifts for a particular age or occasion

- How you believe in your spiritual path

- How you celebrate holidays, and which holidays you observe

- How you dress

- How you raise children

- How you treat the elderly, your parents, your grandparents

- Laws

- Morals you have that come from your family

- Politics

- Routines

- Rules

- What is your philosophy on traditions?

- What traditions have you chosen to no longer uphold? Explain.

- What traditions have you created?

92: TRAVEL & VACATIONS

Travel is going anywhere away from home, but is different from a vacation. A vacation is when you travel to relax and enjoy yourself. Not all family visits are a real vacation. (SEE TOOL SHEETS V: TRAVEL and W: VACATIONS).

- If you have passports, copy them and all the places you have been. Ask for the officials to always stamp your passport so you have a record of when you returned. If you have Global Entry, handwrite your returns on one page. Enter these dates into your CHRONOLOGICAL CALENDAR.

- Trips best and worse

- Adventures

- First trip

- Hotels, those loved and those you would never return to

- Acquaintances and friends you met

- Happenings of all sorts

- Restaurants: food, experiences, and prices

- What you learned from your travels

- Did anyone go with you or meet you?

- The exotic or extraordinary

- Impressive sights and places

- Best/worst experiences

- If I had it to do over again, would I?

- What trips did you take for work that are worth mentioning?

- BUCKET LIST: Where you would like to travel before you "kick the bucket"?

Vacations are trips you plan for fun and relaxation. What memories do you have of going on vacations? Describe each vacation in detail.

- Who went on the vacation? What was their relationship to you?

- What was the destination(s) name(s) and location(s)?

- What was the season?

- What mode(s) of transportation did you travel by?

- What was your budget or expenses?

- What activities did you participate in during the vacation?

- Was there a particular reason for choosing this location?

- What did you enjoy and dislike the most? Explain in detail.

What was the first vacation you planned on your own? Describe in detail.

What vacations and adventures stand out in your mind? What kind of vacation do you prefer? Relaxing, restorative, and quiet? Or do you prefer adventure, exploring, and learning? Who are your favorite people to travel with?

Describe your most memorable vacation and explain why you feel this way.

What are some vacations on your bucket list? See your LIFE CALENDAR.

93: TRUST

In order to function as human beings, we must trust others to some degree. Describe your thoughts, beliefs, and experiences where trust was the issue in both the positive and negative ways. This can be in regard to relationships with professional colleagues, family, and others you are close to.

94: VEHICLES, VESSELS, & VROOM

List all your experiences with vehicles or modes of transportation (See TOOL SHEET X: VEHICLES, VESSELS, & VROOM). Afterwards, add more details about each one.

Remember the childhood anticipation of gaining the privilege to drive and finally having the freedom and independence that comes with it. Often cars and other modes of transportation become either special friends or lemons.

- Who taught you how drive?

- How did your first year of driving go?

- Do you know how to drive both automatic and standard vehicles?

- Have you ever ridden or driven a motorcycle?

- Have you driven a motor boat?

- Have you ever driven a backhoe or heavy equipment?

- Have you ever operated a train?

- Explain what other vehicles you have driven.

Share your stories. Be sure to include the important characters who shared in your adventures and challenges. Include some of the following experiences.

- Accidents

- Back road thumps and bumps

- Breakdowns/running out of gas

- Customs searching or inspecting your car

- Favorites

- Highway adventures

- Maritime emergencies

- Operating a vehicle in a foreign country

- Special trips you took

- Violations and tickets you almost got or were given

- And more ...

95: VOICE—WHEN DID YOU FIND YOUR VOICE?

When was the moment when you found your voice? It can be at different times with different people. What were the circumstances of your experiences? Did you do this gracefully with respect, or did you behave in headstrong and hurtful ways to others to accomplish this?

96: WAR & SERVING YOUR COUNTRY

Some of us have been fortunate not to have experienced war firsthand; others of us have not. Below are some questions for those of you who have experienced living through a war and for those who have served in the armed forces.

ARMED FORCES

Did you serve your country? If so, how did this come about? Did you volunteer, or were you drafted? Did you go to travel or get an education? If you served in the military, please provide the following information and describe the specific situations:

- Enlisted/volunteered or drafted:

- Service number:

- Rank:

- Dates and your age:

- Branch:

- Division:

- Regiment:

- Honors:

- Promotions:

- Benefits:

- Memories of life then:

- Describe the day you enlisted and/or knew you were going.

- Where were you stationed?

- How did it affect you and your family?

- Describe a routine day.

- Describe your uniform and its decoration.

- Describe the daily living conditions, in detail.

WARS & CONFLICTS

- Name of conflict and countries involved:

- Years of conflict:

- How many times were you deployed?

- Your role or involvement:

- Were you ever in direct combat?

- Were you ever wounded?

- How did you transition back to civilian life?

- Have you experienced any issues with post-traumatic stress?

- Have any of your close friends and/or relatives been in active duty?

- What stories have you been told about past wartimes in which your parents or other relatives were involved?

- Have you been married to or involved with someone who is or has been in active service?

97: WISDOM

Wisdom means having knowledge, sagacity, or insight.

- Who do you consider has great wisdom? What is your relationship with this person? Did you know them personally or were they one of the great philosophers?

- From which life experiences have you gained the most wisdom?

- What words of wisdom can you share?

- What life lessons have you learned? Explain in detail.

98: WORDS

Words are fascinating.

As soon as one is able, we are taught to say, "Mama."

We are accused of going through the "terrible twos" because we say, "No!" Yet our parents taught us this very ammunition.

We learn to read the language of our country, then some of us expand and learn other languages.

Words have the most wonderful relationships to other words. We even have names for some of these relationships.

- Homonyms

- Homophones

- Homographs

- Onomatopoeia: words that sound like what they mean, e.g., belch, buzz

- Rhyming words ...

Do you have any words that you love in particular? For example, "Vacuum" with two "U"s or the word "weird" spellings where the "I" does not come before the "E."

Many games are based on words. What are your favorite words in word-making games?

What are your favorite words? What idioms, or commonplace sayings, do you use? What slang words do you use? Have you ever looked into an antique dictionary to find that a word we commonly use today had a totally different meaning? Words are fascinating.

99: WRITINGS YOU HAVE DONE OR WISHED YOU HAD DONE

The art of writing provides a fabulous way to communicate with others, to clarify your thoughts, or to put your feelings down to help you feel better by relieving your mind of things that you feel passionate about (both in a good and bad way).

- Has writing been a part of your life? What is your pattern of writing? Seldom? Frequently? Daily? What motivates you to want to write? Is your writing fiction, non-fiction, technical? What topics do you like to write about? How do you discipline yourself to write?

- What authors do you love to read? In particular, what books or articles are of interest to you?

- Who has influenced your writing the most?

- Include some of your writings.

- What writings are still in the back of your mind that you have not finished or have not started?

- Did you ever have a language you created before being taught your parents' language?

100: YOUR QUESTIONS TO ADD

Now that you have an understanding of this book, what would you like to add?

PART III: TOOL SHEETS A-Z

TOOL SHEET A: ACTIVITIES, HOBBIES, INTERESTS, COLLECTIBLES, & SPORTS

(SPORTS below)

Read each entry below and jot your memories that come to you. Then write about the ones that had the most meaning.

21 Questions	Beading/beadwork	Canasta
Acey Deucey (cards)	Billiards	Candles
Acting	Bird feathers	Candlesticks
Antique cars	Birding	Carpentry
Antiques	Blogging	Cars
Antiquing	Book restoration	Carving
Art	Books	Ceramics
Art collecting	Board games	Checkers
Artwork	Bridge	Cheerleading
Astrology	Bumper cars	Chess
Backgammon	Butterfly watching	China
Ballet	Buttons	Chinese checkers
Batik	Calligraphy	Cigars
Battleship	Cameras	Cigarette holders
Beachcombing	Camping	Clay

Cloud watching

Coins

Collages

Collecting gems

Comic books

Computer

Coffee roasting

Cooking

Coloring

Couponing

Creative writing

Cribbage

Crocheting

Cross-stitching

Crossword puzzles

Cryptography

Crystals

Dance

Debate

Digital arts

Doll houses

Dominoes

Dowsing

Drama

Drawing

Dried flowers

Driving

Eating out

Educational pursuits

Electronics

Embroidery

Enameling

Engraving

Entertaining

Fantasy sports

Fashion

Flower arranging

Films

Fish (cards)

Fish Tank

Food critic

Foreign language

Flying

Fossils & rocks

Gambling

Gardening

Genealogy

Geocaching

Ghost hunting

Gin rummy

Glassblowing

Graffiti art

Gunsmithing

Hand analysis

Hearts (cards game)

Herbing

Home repair

Home brewing

Hot air ballooning

Ice skating

Insect collecting

Interior decorating

Internet browsing

Jewelry making

Jigsaw puzzles

Jotto

Journaling

Juggling

Kite flying

Knitting

Lace making

Learning

Listening to music	Pottery	Spelunking
Macramé	Print making	Spite and Malice (cards)
Magic	Puppetry	
Marbles	Puzzles	Stained glass making
Match strikers	Quilting	Stamps
Metal detecting	Quotes	Stargazing
Metalworking	Reading	Stationery
Meteorology	Relaxing	Storytelling
Models	Rocks	Tarot card reading
Music	Rummikub	Taxidermy
Musical instruments	Rummy	Teaching
Needlepoint	Scrapbooking	Television watching
Old maid	Sculpting	Theater
Opera	Sea glass	Tombstone rubbing
Origami	Seashells	Tools
Painting	Sewing	Travel
Pens	Shooting	Trivia
People watching	Shopping	Umbrella collecting
Pets	Singing	Vehicle restoration
Photographs	Sketching	Video games
Photography	Sleeping	Vintage cars
Playing instrument	Smoking	Volunteering
Poker	Socializing	Walking
Postcards	Software	War (cards)

Watching movies

Watching sports

Welding

Whale watching

Wine

Woodworking

Writing

SPORTS

Archery

Auto racing

Badminton

Baseball

Basketball

Beach volleyball

Biking

Billiards

Boating

Bobsledding/Luge

Body building

Bowling

Boxing

Bull riding

Bullfighting

Canoeing

Car racing

Climbing

Cricket

Croquet

Cross country skiing

Curling

Cycling

Dancing

Darts

Dressage

Diving

Dodgeball

Dog racing

Exercising

Fencing

Figure skating

Field hockey

Fishing

Flying discs

Football

Four-wheeling

Fox hunting

Frisbee

Game hunting

Geocaching

Golf

Gymnastics

Hang gliding

Handball

Hiking

Horseback riding

Horse racing

Horse shows

Hunting

Ice hockey

Ice skating

Judo

Karate

Kayaking

Kickboxing

Lacrosse

Marathons (racing)

Martial arts

Meditation

Miniature golf

Motorcross

Motorcycle riding	Roller skating	Swimming
Mountain biking	Rowing	Table tennis
Mountain climbing	Rugby	Team sports
Olympic sports	Running	Tennis
Paddle boarding	Sailing	Track and field
Paddle tennis	Sculling	Trampoline
Paddleball	Shooting	Trap shooting
Parachuting	Skateboarding	Unicycling
Pentathlon	Skating	Volleyball
Ping pong	Skeet shooting	Walking
Polo	Ski jumping	Water polo
Pool	Skiing	Waterskiing
Racquetball	Skydiving	Weightlifting
Rafting	Snorkeling	Whale watching
Rally	Snowboarding	Windsurfing
Road biking	Snowmobiling	Wrestling
Rodeo	Softball	Yoga
Roller derby	Squash	
Roller hockey	Surfing	

TOOL SHEET B: ANIMALS & CRITTERS

Write about each of the animals & critters you have owned, experienced in a significant way.

Animal type:

Breed:

Height & Weight:

Name:

Date acquired:

Date of death/departure:

Description:

Memoirs:

TOOL SHEET C: CAMPS I HAVE ATTENDED

Write about each camp you have attended.

Name:

Address:

Year/s attended:

Length of camp stay:

Reason for going:

Memoirs:

Activities:

Special events:

Friends there or made new:

Accomplishments:

Decisions you made:

Typical activities:

Rules:

Embarrassments:

Favorite counselor:

People you didn't especially like:

Were you homesick, and if so, how did you cope with it?

Did you receive snail mail or care packages? Do you have any old letters? Were you allowed to have electronic communications?

Favorite memories:

TOOL SHEET D: CHARACTERISTICS OF STRENGTHS & CHALLENGES

Below are some characteristics of people, both the strengths and the challenges. When you first read this list, write the name of anyone (including yourself) who comes to mind. You may even see a pattern with the kinds of people you attract into your life. This list will bring up people who you may have not thought about in years (Also see TOOL SHEET A: ACTIVITIES, HOBBIES, INTERESTS, COLLECTIBLES, & SPORTS). (Original list came from Peter Orgain of South Strafford, Vermont.)

Abusive	Analytical
Achievement-oriented	Angry
Active	Anxious
Acts out emotions	Apologetic
Adaptable	Appreciative
Addicted to "doingness"	Approachable
Adventurous	Arrogant
Aesthetically oriented	Artistic
Affectionate	Athletic
Aggressive	Attractive
Alert	Beautiful
Aloof	Begrudging
Ambitious	Bigoted

Boastful

Bored by details

Bossy

Boundaries issues

Brave

Broad-minded

Businesslike

Can be inflexible in control mode

Can be unwilling to connect

Caring

Challenging, meaningful work

Comfortable with life

Contributes to family relationships

Creative, interesting, engaging work

Closed minded

Combative

Compulsive

Competitive

Confident

Conscientious

Considerate

Constructive ideas

Contemplative

Conventional

Creative

Critical, but not always judging

Cultured

Decisive

Deep

Demonstrative

Dependable

Detail-minded

Determined

Difficulty relaxing

Dignified

Disciplined

Dishonest

Disorganized

Distant

Does not speak clearly

Does not speak from the heart

Does not vent emotions in conflicts

Does not admit or see own mistakes

Does not nurture peer relationships

Dramatic

Eccentric

Economical

Emotional

Emotionally detached

Empathetic

Energetic

Enjoyable to work with

Enterprising

Enthusiastic

Environmentally aware

Evades responsibility

Evasive

Exacting

Excitable

Extravagant

Extroverted

Family-oriented

Feels productive

Feels safe and secure

Financially responsible

Financially secure

Focused

Formal

Frank

Free time (creates time to play)

Friendly

Fulfilling friendships

Fulfilling marital and/or family life

Focused on what is to be achieved

Follows the rules

Funny

Fussy

Generous

Gentle

Good memory

Good natured

Good person

Greedy

Gregarious

Happy

Hardworking

Harmonious

Helpful

Honest

Honorable

Humiliates other people

Humorless

Humorous

Idealistic

Ignorant

Imaginative

Impatient

Inability to tolerate negatives

Inability to work under pressure

Inarticulate

Incongruent (does not walk the talk)

Independent

Individualistic

Inefficient

Inflexible

Inspiring

Insulting

Intellectual

Intimidating behavior towards others

Intolerant

Introvert (being with people is exhausting)

Intuitive

Irrational

Irritable

Invalidating of others

Jealous

Jovial

Judgmental

Keen foresight

Kind

Lacks awareness

Lashes out

Leadership qualities

Leaving the world/job a better place

Liar

Lively

Long-winded

Loving

Loyal

Lucky

Manipulative

Mentoring

Methodical

Motivated

Mutual respect with others

Narcissistic

Natural

Nervous

Non-communicative

Not overloaded life

Nurturing with self and others

Observant

Open-minded

Opinionated

Optimistic

Organized

Original

Outdoorsy

Outgoing

Outspoken

Overbearing

Overcommitted

Overly emotional

Overprotective

Passive aggressive

Pensive

Perfectionist-minded

Personal growth-oriented

Petty

Philosophical

Playful

Pleasant

Poetic

Poor at completing things fully or well

Positive

Practical

Prejudiced

Pretty

Prideful

Private

Productive

Professional

Protective

Proud

Purposeful

Quick-minded

Racist

Rapid mind

Realistic

Relaxed

Reliable

Resistant to change

Resourceful

Respectful

Responsible

Restless

Romantic

Sarcastic

Savvy

Secretive

Secure

Self-aware of behaviors and feelings

Self-critical to an excessive degree

Self-motivated

Self-satisfaction with your behaviors and feelings

Self-reliant

Sensitive

Sentimental

Serious

Service-oriented

Sexist

Sexy

Shallow

Shy

Sincere

Skeptical

Slow decision maker

Smart

Sociable

Social contributions to society

Sophisticated

Spiritual connection

Spontaneous

Stern

Strong

Stubborn

Super parent

Supportive

Systematic

Tactful

Tactless

Talkative

Team player

Tender-hearted

Thorough

Thoughtful

Thoughtless

Tidy

Time-stressed

Timely communicator

Trusting

Trustworthy

Truthful

Unaware

Unbalanced life/habits

Uncomfortable with conflicts

Understanding

Unforgiving about mistakes

Unhealthy

Unique

Unresponsive

Unstable

Untruthful

Venting emotions in conflicts

Vindictive

Violent

Visionary

Vulnerable to manipulation by others

Wanton

Weak/prone to addictions

Well-adjusted

Well-intentioned

Well-mannered

Workaholic

Young-minded

Zealous

TOOL SHEET E: CLOTHING & FASHION

When did you become conscientious of fashion?

Did you feel pressure to conform or need to be different?

What were the popular fads when you were growing up?

Who were the famous models/designers of your favorite time?

What were your favorite colors/styles?

Do you know if your skin type is winter, spring, summer, or fall?

What were the prices of clothing? How much did you spend on clothing? (Include receipts if possible. Include your ledger or budget reports on how much you actually spent on clothing).

Do you have photographs to show how times have changed in the clothing industry? Yearbooks and photos are good sources. Take photos of your outfits now and over the next years.

Include some photos of current fashions. Include hairstyles, clothing, shoes, eyeglasses, and makeup.

Other memories:

FASHION by DECADE

1901-1910	1971-1980
1911-1920	1981-1990
1921-1930	1991-2000
1931-1940	2001-2010
1941-1950	2011-2020
1951-1960	2021-2030
1961-1970	2031-2040

TOOL SHEET F: DEATH

Name of person/animal:

Relationship to you:

Date of death:

Their age:

Your age:

Cause of death:

Funeral or services:

How did you first meet/come together?

Were you nearby at the time of death?

Do you have any mementos or gifts from them?

Best memories of the times you shared with this person/animal:

Have you experienced their presence since their passing?

Medical history:

What will always trigger your memory to remind you of them?

How did this person's/animal's passing affect you?

What are the funniest, happiest, or favorite things you remember about the deceased?

Other memories:

TOOL SHEET G: EDUCATION

Name of institution:

Address:

Distance from home:

Years attended:

Degree conferred:

Number of students at institution:

Number of students per class:

Number of faculty:

Public or private:

Tuition per year:

Areas of concentration:

Minor concentrations:

Honors, awards, elections:

Extra-curricular activities:

Student employment:

Why was this institution chosen?

Favorite areas of study (or least favorite)?

Describe a typical day.

Any favorite teachers/professors?

What were your average grades?

Were there other people who inspired you?

Did you play sports?

Did you have an IEP (Individualized Education Plan)? Did you have any diagnosed learning challenges (Dyslexia, etc.)?

What tests have you had?

Description of campus:

Do you still keep in contact with faculty/friends?

Do you participate in alumni activities?

Any other memories/thoughts?

TOOL SHEET H: EMPLOYMENT, SELF-EMPLOYMENT, & EMPLOYEES

INCLUDES 3 SECTIONS

SECTION 1: WORK PERFORMED FOR AN EMPLOYER

Company:

Employer:

Position:

Address:

Dates of Employment:

How old were you?

Wages per week:

Benefits:

Social Security rate: Employer %:   Employee %:

Tax rate: Federal %:   State %:

How did you feel about the work and the environment?

SECTION 2: SELF-EMPLOYMENT HISTORY

Company:

Company name:

Location:

Address:

Date first founded:

How old were you?

What were your earnings per week?

Employed others?

How many employees?

Currently operational?

Why did you start this business?

What is the current status of your business? If closed, explain what happened.

SECTION 3: EMPLOYEES

Name:

Your company name at the time and the nature of the business:

Was this person a domestic employee? Did he/she live at your residence?

Job performed in detail:

Pay:

How long was this person employed by you?

How was their performance?

TOOL SHEET I: ENVIRONMENT

MAPS OF WHERE I HAVE LIVED & TRAVELED

Illustrate or show maps of the different places you have lived. You can obtain satellite pictures through the Internet of where you lived in both "Landscape" and "Map" view using the satellite maps to show the layout of your properties and neighborhoods. Mark the maps of all the places you have lived, the dates you lived there and your age at the time.

Permanent markers are the best tools for this, so your markings do not fade over time.

SPECIAL PLACES

Do you have special memories of places that you have visited? Which places are these and why are they special to you? Do you ever go back to visit these places? Is there anyone there that remembers you? Have these places changed much over time?

FLOOR PLANS

Draw a floor map of your room growing up. Make another map or floor plan of your houses and properties where you have lived for a period of time. (Often you can find the footprint in any appraisal documents through your insurance company. If you built your home, you could ask your architect for scanned copies of the blueprints.)

SCRIBBLE OR DRAW BELOW:

TOOL SHEET J: FAMILY HISTORY

To help find some of the information needed to complete this Tool Sheet, you could check with public records, such as civil registration, church, cemetery, census, probate, military, and immigration records. Keep in mind that some of your ancestors may have changed the spelling of their names, created spelling variations, and made errors in handwritten documents.

YOURSELF

Name:

Familiar name/nick names:

DOB:

Location of birth:

Do you desire cremation or burial? Do you have a plot?

FATHER

Name:

Familiar name/nick names:

DOB:

Location of birth:

DOD and cause:

Cremation/burial and location of remains:

MOTHER

Name:

Familiar name/nick names:

DOB:

Location of birth:

DOD and cause:

Cremation/burial and location of remains:

GRANDPARENTS

Name: DOB:

Name: DOB:

Name: DOB:

Name: DOB:

SIBLINGS

Name: DOB:

Name: DOB:

Name: DOB:

Name: DOB:

Name: DOB:

Name: DOB:

Name: DOB:

Name: DOB:

Name: DOB:

CHILDREN

Name: DOB:

Name: DOB:

Name: DOB:

Name: DOB:

Name: DOB:

Name: DOB:

Name: DOB:

GRANDCHILDREN

Name: DOB:

Name: DOB:

Name: DOB:

Name: DOB:

Name: DOB:

Name: DOB:

Name: DOB:

Name: DOB:

Name: DOB:

Name: DOB:

Name: DOB:

Name: DOB:

Name: DOB:

Name: DOB:

Name: DOB:

Name: DOB:

Memories relating to your home and the environment (sensory):

Memories relating to your family:

Favorite or best memories?

Worst memories?

Stories about your siblings, parents, and you:

Special places or hiding places:

Memories of times of sorrow (emotional, physical, environmental, spiritual):

Diseases and illnesses (see TOOL SHEET L: HEALTH RECORDS):

STEP-PARENTS

Name: DOB:

Name: DOB:

STEP-GRANDPARENTS

Name: DOB:

Name: DOB:

Name: DOB:

Name: DOB:

STEPCHILDREN

Name: DOB:

Name: DOB:

Name: DOB:

Name: DOB:

Name: DOB:

Name: DOB:

Name: DOB:

Name: DOB:

STEP-SIBLINGS

Name: DOB:

Name: DOB:

Name: DOB:

Name: DOB:

Name: DOB:

Name: DOB:

Name: DOB:

Memories relating to your stepfamily:

How old were they when you met them?

Did they live with you full-time or part-time?

Did you and your stepfamily get along?

Stories about your stepfamily:

Diseases and illnesses (see TOOL SHEET L: HEALTH RECORDS).

TOOL SHEET K: FAMILY TREE

Having a family tree is such a wonderful treat. How many generations you go back will determine the number of pages needed. There are online resources to help you as well. Start by sketching your immediate family tree. Then add if you have step-family members. Usually a family tree includes information for each person: Date of Birth, Date of Marriage, Children that resulted from marriages, Date of Divorce (if applicable), and finally Date of Death.

YOUR TREE HERE

TOOL SHEET L: HEALTH RECORDS

List your family members. Include all documents you can find (See TOOL SHEET J: FAMILY HISTORY).

- Birth certificates

- Baby footprints

- Adoption papers

- Immunization records

- Birth records from doctors and hospitals

- Include other health records

- What genetic diseases run in your family? Add details.

- Is there a history of cancer? Add details.

- Is there a history of mental illness? Add details.

- Have there been any miscarriages or infant deaths? Explain.

- Is there a history of addiction? Add details.

- Other facts:

TOOL SHEET M: INVENTORY

Record information about personal belongings of importance.

Item:

Type of item:

Size:

Price/worth when you got it:

Present value:

Present location:

Where it came from:

Photograph:

What does it personally mean to you?

TOOL SHEET N: LEGAL FACTS

Describe a legal situation in which you have been involved:

Who was the plaintiff?

Who was the defendant?

Did you hire an attorney?

If so, what was the name of your attorney?

Date started:

How long did the involvement take to settle?

Describe the situation:

What was the outcome?

What did you learn and what would you advise others?

Include wills, trusts, and other legal documents:

Share your thoughts about your legal situations.

TOOL SHEET O: LESSONS & CLASSES WITH INSTRUCTION

Type of lesson:

How old were you?

How many years did you take these lessons?

Did you request these lessons or did your parents insist?

How passionate were you about these lessons?

Did these lessons influence your choice of career?

Did you follow through with additional lessons as an adult?

Are there lessons you wished you had taken? If you did not follow through, what prevented you from doing so?

TOOL SHEET P: MARRIAGE, ENGAGEMENT, SIGNIFICANT OTHERS, SEPARATION, & DIVORCE

<u>First Marriage/Union:</u>

Name of spouse:

DOB/death:

Date of wedding:

Service:

Officiated by:

Location:

Type of wedding:

Number of guests:

Attendants:

Rings exchanged (describe):

Tokens of love given between bride and groom:

Attire worn:

Music:

Photographer:

Reception:

Rehearsal dinner:

Cost and paid by whom?

Memories of the day, food, festivities:

Engagement: Describe the event of becoming engaged:

Second Marriage/Union:

Name of spouse:

DOB/death:

Date of wedding:

Service:

Officiated by:

Location:

Type of wedding:

Number of guests:

Attendants:

Rings exchanged (describe):

Tokens of love given between bride and groom:

Attire worn:

Music:

Photographer:

Reception:

Rehearsal dinner:

Cost and paid by whom?

Memories of the day, food, festivities:

Engagement: Describe the event of becoming engaged:

Divorce:

Name of spouse;

Date of divorce:

Reason for divorce:

Were there children? How old were the children when divorce was initiated?

How long did the divorce take to become final?

Who was your lawyer? How did you feel about your lawyer's performance?

Did it go to court?

What did you learn? How would you advise others as a result of your experience?

TOOL SHEET Q: MUSIC & DANCE

Write about the importance of music and dance in your life.

- Do you play an instrument(s)? If so, which ones?

- Have you had lessons? Who was your teacher?

- Do you sing? If so, do you sing solo, or with a group such as a choir? Have you had lessons?

- Do you like to listen to music? Live or recorded?

- Which genres of music do you enjoy?

- Did you have exposure to music while growing up?

- Has your taste in music changed?

- Have you had dancing lessons? Who was your teacher?

- Do you dance today? How important is dancing in your life?

- What cultural music and dancing do you love?

- What is your experience of going other places to be exposed to music and dance?

- What are your favorite songs and dances?

- Have you ever written a song?

TOOL SHEET R: NATURE

What experiences or living situations have you had with nature? Explain in detail including your ages and the years.

What is your relationship with nature? What does nature do for your inner soul?

Have you had any employment around nature?

What memberships do you have, or what organizations do you belong to that involve nature?

What traveling have you done around nature?

Memoirs:

TOOL SHEET S: PEOPLE

This tool sheet is for you to record particular faces that pop into mind, those with whom you shared particular experiences, have left impressions for better or worse, and shared certain philosophies. Include family, friends, employers, employees, teachers, acquaintances, fellow travelers, and those who are quirky and unique (See TOOL SHEET D: CHARACTERISTS OF STRENGTHS & CHALLENGES).

Name:

When did you meet?

Relationship to you:

How did you meet?

First impression:

What characteristics made this person stand out to you?

What experiences and memoirs have you shared?

TOOL SHEET T: REAL ESTATE

Real Estate—BUILDING I

Address:

Name given to property:

Dates owned/rented/leased:

Lot size:

Historical aspects:

Square footage of building:

Number of rooms:

Number of bedrooms:

Number of bathrooms:

Style of building:

Amenities:

Pool or game area:

Outbuildings:

Media rooms:

Art studio:

Garage:

Suburban, country, or urban setting:

Did you have a mortgage? If so, what was the interest rate?

Septic or sewer?

Personal or business property?

Purchase price:

Selling price:

How long did it take you to find this property?

What were your wants and requirements in searching for this property?

How did you become aware that this property was for sale?

Reasons (determining factors) for purchasing/selling property and determining factors

Did you purchase this real estate by yourself or with a partner?

Describe the building (number of rooms, yard/land, special features, architecture, type of heating, lighting):

On another piece of paper, draw floor plans of the buildings and survey a diagram of the yard.

Explain why you moved and the effect it had on you and your family. What were the difficulties encountered and what did you learn?

What was different about this location from where you were before?

Real Estate—BUILDING II

Address:

Name given to property:

Dates owned/rented/leased:

Lot size:

Historical aspects:

Square footage of building:

Number of rooms:

Number of bedrooms:

Number of bathrooms:

Style of building:

Amenities:

Pool:

Outbuildings:

Media rooms:

Art studio:

Garage:

Suburban, country, or urban setting:

Did you have a mortgage? If so, what was the interest rate?

Septic or sewer?

Personal or business property?

Purchase price:

Selling price:

How long did it take you to find this property?

What were your wants and requirements in searching for this property?

How did you become aware that this property was for sale?

Reasons (determining factors) for purchasing/selling property and determining factors

Did you purchase this real estate by yourself or with a partner?

Describe the building (number of rooms, yard/land, special features, architecture, type of heating, lighting):

On another piece of paper, draw floor plans of the buildings and survey a diagram of the yard.

Explain why you moved and the effect it had on you and your family. What were the difficulties encountered and what did you learn?

What was different about this location from where you were before?

Real Estate—OFFICES

Address:

Name given to property or business:

Dates owned/rented/leased:

Lot size:

Historical aspects:

Square footage of building:

Number of rooms:

Number of bathrooms:

Style of building:

Amenities:

Pool:

Outbuildings:

Secondary buildings:

Suburban, country, or urban setting?

Did you have a mortgage? Interest rate? Rent?

Septic or sewer?

Personal or business property?

Purchase price:

Selling price:

How long did it take you to find this property?

What were your specifications and requirements in searching for this property?

How did you become aware that this property was for sale?

Reason (determining factors) for purchasing/selling property:

Did you purchase this real estate by yourself or with a partner?

Describe the building (number of rooms, yard/land, special features, architecture, type of heating, lighting)

On another piece of paper, draw floor plans of the buildings and a diagram of the yard.

What was different about this location from where you were before?

TOOL SHEET U: RELIGION

Parent 1 religious faith:

Parent 2 religious faith:

How do you define your religious beliefs? Do you consider yourself a religious person?

Was there a religious ceremony performed when you were born to formalize your religious affiliation?

If you have children, have you introduced formal religious education in their lives?

What were the dates of your religious events and festivities?

Are there any interesting historical facts about your family regarding religion?

Do you have godparents? If so, why were they chosen? What is their relationship to your parents and where do they live now?

Who were the most influential people in your life regarding your religious upbringing?

If you are not practicing a formal religion, do you consider yourself a spiritual person? What is the nature of your spirituality?

Are you an atheist? If so how did you decide this?

TOOL SHEET V: TRAVEL

Where have you traveled? If you have a passport(s) copy them and all the places you have been. Ask for the border/customs officers to always stamp your passport so you have a record. If you have Global Entry, handwrite your returns on one page. Enter these dates into your CHRONOLOGICAL CALENDAR.

What year did you travel?

How old were you?

With whom did you travel?

Reason for the trip?

Business, vacation, visiting family or friends, military service?

Did you keep a journal?

Have you gone back or do you hope to return?

Mementos:

Purchases:

Type of transportation:

Sights you saw:

What did you learn on this trip? Special memories? Include photos, letters, postcards and journals.

TOOL SHEET W: VACATIONS

Tell about vacations you have taken.

Where did your vacation take place?

What year was it?

How old were you?

With whom did you take this vacation?

How long was it?

Did you keep a journal?

Would you go back again?

Special memories? Include photos, letters, and journals.

TOOL SHEET X: VEHICLES, VESSELS, & VROOM

List all the vehicles and other modes of transportation you have owned/operated (automobiles, motorcycles, boats, planes, jet skis, backhoes, tractors, four-wheelers, golf carts, planes, bicycles, ATVs, carriages, etc.).

Vehicle make and model:

Year manufactured:

Date acquired and price:

Improvements or repairs:

Nickname for the vehicle and story behind this:

Date sold and price:

Description: color, condition, standard or automatic transmission?

Memoirs in detail (Please write the date of the adventure, your age at the time, and the date you wrote this answer).

Charlotte Donaldson

TOOL SHEET Y: VOCATIONS

Read the words below and jot down the memories they bring to you.
Then write about your favorite ones.

Accountant	Bank teller	Carpenter
Acrobat	Barber	Cartoonist
Actor	Bartender	Chauffeur
Acupuncturist	Beautician	Chemist
Animal trainer	Biochemist	Chiropractor
Antique specialist	Boat captain	Choreographer
Appraiser	Bodyguard	College professor
Archeologist	Bookbinder	Comedian
Architect	Book editor	Composer
Artist	Botanist	Computer specialist
Athlete (professional)	Bricklayer	Concierge
Attorney	Bridge inspector	Conductor
Auditor	Building inspector	Construction inspector
Author	Butcher	Contractor
Automobile mechanic	Buyer	Cook/Chef
Automobile racer	Cabinetmaker	Copywriter
Baker	Cake decorator	Costumer
	Cardiologist	Counselor
	Caretaker	

Court Clerk

Curator

Customs inspector

Dancer

Day care worker

Dental hygienist

Deputy

Dermatologist

Detective

Dietitian

Diver

Drama coach

Dressmaker

Driver

Editor

Educational specialist

Electrician

Engineer

Engraver

Entrepreneur

Environmentalist

Equestrian

Estate planner

Excavator

Exterminator

Fabric designer

Farmer/Rancher

Fire fighter

Fish farmer

Flight attendant

Floralist

Food tester

Forester

Fumigator

Fundraiser

Funeral home director

Gamekeeper

Geographer

Geologist

Glass blower

Golf club manager

Government official

Greenhouse manager

Gunsmith

Hair Stylist

Headwaiter/waitress

Heating and air conditioning mechanic

Heavy equipment operator

Historian

Homemaker

Housekeeper

Illustrator

Inspector

Interior designer

Interpreter

Investigator

Janitor

Jeweler

Jockey

Judge

Knitter

Laboratory technician

Landscape gardener

Lawyer

Legislator

Librarian

Lifeguard

Lobsterman

Locksmith

Magician

Maid

Mathematician

Mechanic

Medical scientist

Meteorologist

Mime

Miner

Musician

Nanny

Narrator

Navigator

Neurologist

Nurse

Obstetrician

Operations supervisor

Optician

Optometrist

Painter

Patent agent

Pathologist

Pediatrician

Perfumer

Periodontist

Personal shopper

Pharmacist

Photojournalist

Photographer

Physiatrist

Physician

Physiologist

Pilot

Playwright

Plumber

Poet

Police officer

Politician

Postmaster

President

Printmaker

Property manager

Psychiatrist

Radio announcer

Radiologist

Ranger

Real estate agent

Receptionist

Restorer

Roofer

Safari guide

Sales clerk

Salesperson

School principal

Screen writer

Scuba diver

Sculptor

Secretary

Ship captain

Shoe repairer

Silversmith

Singer

Social worker

Stage director

Stone carver

Stonemason

Surgeon

Surveyor

Tarot reader

Teacher

Town clerk

Translator

Travel guide	Waiter/Waitress	Wholesaler
Tutor	Watch repairer	Wildlife manager
Umpire	Weaver	Wine maker
Upholsterer	Wedding consultant	Writer
Veterinarian	Welder	

TOOL SHEET Z: VOLUNTEER WORK

List all volunteer work you have performed.

Organization:

National or international?

Location:

Dates of involvement:

How old were you?

Was it required to satisfy an obligation or complete a degree?

How did your interest in this work develop? How did you feel about the work and the environment?

Organization:

National or international?

Location:

Dates of involvement:

How old were you?

Was it required to satisfy an obligation or complete a degree?

How did your interest in this work develop? How did you feel about the work and the environment?

Made in the USA
Columbia, SC
03 October 2023

23838824R00150